5 Keys to Business Analytics Program Success

John Boyer
Bill Frank
Brian Green
Tracy Harris
Kay Van De Vanter

MC Press Online, LLC
Boise, ID 83703

5 Keys to Business Analytics Program Success

John Boyer, Bill Frank, Brian Green, Tracy Harris, Kay Van De Vanter

First Edition
First Printing — October 2012

MC Press offers excellent discounts on this book when ordered in quantity for bulk purchases or special sales, which may include custom covers and content particular to your business, training goals, marketing focus, and branding interest.

MC Press Online, LLC
    Corporate Offices
    3695 W Quail Heights Court
    Boise, ID 83703-3861 USA

For information regarding sales and/or customer service, please contact:
    MC Press
    P.O. Box 4300
    Big Sandy, TX 75755-4300 USA

For information regarding permissions or special orders, please contact:
    mcbooks@mcpressonline.com

ISBN: 978-1-58347-343-6

Acknowledgments

We would like to thank Les Rechan and Mychelle Mollot of the Business Analytics division of IBM® for sponsoring this book and providing the support to make it happen. We would also like to thank the management teams, colleagues, and knowledge experts at BlueCross BlueShield of Tennessee, The Boeing Company, Johnson & Johnson, RCG Global Services, DaimlerTrucks North America, Elie Tahari, Martin's Point Health Care, Mueller, The Nielsen Company, and AlignAlytics for all their hard work in seeing this project through to completion. Without the combined work, support, advice, and knowledge of these teams, *5 Keys to Business Analytics Program Success* would not have been possible.

About the Authors

The content for this book was prepared by the IBM Business Analytics Excellence Advisory Board, a team of representatives from leading enterprise organizations who research, advise, and share best practices for achieving excellence in Business Analytics initiatives.

John Boyer

John Boyer is Director, Business Intelligence and Data Warehousing, RCG Global Services. Previously, he led software development and enablement of custom BI software for The Nielsen Company. At Nielsen, John was a key member of the BI COE, where he managed the BI Advisory Team that oversaw adoption, enablement, and internal consulting for all things BI. Before joining Nielsen, John spent several years as a BI architect and trusted advisor at IBM. After graduating from medical school, his aptitude, passion, and bedside manner took him first to a healthcare clinic, where he rose to Director of Finance and Information Systems.

John has spent the past 17 years consulting in software development, business analytics, and data warehousing. He is past-chair of the Illinois Cognos User Group. As an IBM Information Champion, he has been invited to speak and conduct workshops at a number of national events, including Information on Demand, Cognos Forum, Cognos User Groups, and the Composite Software annual conference.

About RCG Global Services

RCG Global Services (*www.rcggs.com*) has a rich 38-year history of providing professional services to the Global 1000 marketplace. The company has developed a repeatable blueprint to affect business change that typically involves the application of technology. Its technology design and implementation follow a rigorous, predictable approach that ensures a customized solution tailored to the client. Headquartered in Edison, New Jersey, USA, with 12 offices throughout the United States, RCG has more than 1,500 consultants with an average of 14 years of experience. RCG serves more than 360 clients, including 43 of the Fortune 100, with a focus on the insurance, healthcare, retail, energy, and entertainment industries. RCG was named to the Global Services 100 list of companies in 2011 for the third year in a row for outstanding Global Delivery Maturity.

Bill Frank

Bill Frank is Manager, ITGF BI Practice, at Johnson & Johnson. He has more than 25 years of experience in information technology. Bill is a Project Management Professional (PMP) and a Certified Business Intelligence Professional (CBIP). He has held positions of varying responsibility in the DSS/BI space at major companies, including AT&T, Verizon, Time Warner AOL, and Johnson & Johnson. At J&J, Bill has played key roles in the development of BI solutions, technology selection and standardization, organizational models, proven practices, and evangelizing BI across the enterprise. Bill is a founding member of the J&J BI Community of Practice and leads this 200+ member internal group focused on leverage, communication, and sharing practices and strategies.

Bill played critical roles in efforts at J&J that led to the creation of the IBM Cognos Enterprise Agreement, Shared BI Environments, and an Enterprise DW strategy. These initiatives are key to supporting J&J's standardization, rationalization, and consolidation efforts. Currently, Bill is developing strategies for the Enterprise DW at J&J with a focus on a CPM solution for the Office of Finance. He is a member of the IBM BI Excellence Advisory Board. Bill lives in New Jersey and has four children. His interests include playing guitar, golf, and cooking.

About Johnson & Johnson

Johnson & Johnson (*www.jnj.com*) is a Fortune 100™ company, encompassing the world's premier consumer health company, the world's largest and most diverse medical devices and diagnostics company, fourth-largest biologics company, and eighth-largest pharmaceuticals company. J&J has more than 250 operating companies in 60 countries and employs approximately 114,000 people. The company is headquartered in New Brunswick, New Jersey.

Brian Green

Brian Green is Manager of Business Intelligence and Performance Management at BlueCross BlueShield of Tennessee. He has more than 30 years of information management and system development experience in the insurance industry, with expertise in process improvement and organizational development to align delivery of solutions with business strategy. Brian is also working with local business and academic leaders to build an Information Management and Business Analytics curriculum with the goal of developing the Business Intelligence leaders of tomorrow.

About BlueCross and BlueShield of Tennessee

BlueCross BlueShield of Tennessee (*www.bcbst.com*) offers its clients peace of mind through affordable solutions for health and healing, life and living. Founded in 1945, the Chattanooga, Tennessee-based company is focused on reinventing the health plan for its three million members. Through its integrated health management approach, BlueCross develops patient-centric products and services that positively impact affordability, patient safety, and quality. BlueCross BlueShield of Tennessee, Inc., is an independent licensee of the BlueCross BlueShield Association.

Tracy Harris

Tracy Harris is Senior Manager, Business Analytics Excellence, at IBM. She is responsible for chairing the BA Excellence Advisory Board and managing the Business Analytics Excellence Program and Champion initiative at IBM. These programs are designed to help organizations achieve success, business value, and excellence in their BA and performance management initiatives and are defined through the sharing of best practices, research, and guidance from industry leaders and subject-matter experts. Tracy has worked with Fortune 500® organizations and government organizations around the globe to gather and research best practices in achieving excellence, and she shares this research through workshops and speaking engagements worldwide on the topic.

About IBM

International Business Machines Corporation (*www.ibm.com*) is one of the world's largest technology companies—a multinational computer, technology, and IT consulting corporation headquartered in Armonk, New York. IBM manufactures and sells computer hardware and software and offers infrastructure services, hosting services, and consulting services in areas ranging from mainframe computers to nanotechnology. With nearly 400,000 employees worldwide and sales of more than 100 billion U.S. dollars, IBM holds more patents than any other U.S. technology company and operates eight research laboratories worldwide. The company has scientists, engineers, consultants, and sales professionals in over 200 countries. IBM employees have earned five Nobel Prizes, four Turing Awards, nine National Medals of Technology, and five National Medals of Science.

Kay Van De Vanter

Kay Van De Vanter is the enterprise BI architect for The Boeing Company, with more than 12 years of experience in IT and business intelligence areas. For the past several years, she has led Boeing's Business Intelligence Competency Center team and has worked with several other key information management teams to drive the standardization and alignment of BI initiatives at Boeing. Kay has also collaborated with industry BI professionals, user groups, and teams to help drive innovation and quality in the BI tools used by Boeing. She is currently partnering with others to develop an enterprise BI and technology strategy in support of Boeing's business goals. Kay is a member of IBM's BI Excellence Advisory Board and BI Customer Advisory Board, co-chair of the Seattle Cognos User Group as well as other external groups focused on BI technologies and best practices.

About The Boeing Company

The Boeing Company (*www.boeing.com*) is the world's largest aerospace company and leading manufacturer of commercial jetliners and defense, space, and security systems. Boeing products and tailored services include commercial and military aircraft, satellites, weapons, electronic and defense systems, launch systems, advanced information and communications systems, and performance-based logistics and training. Boeing's Engineering, Operations, and Technology business unit supports the company's business units by delivering high-quality, low-cost technical services in IT, research and technology, and test and evaluation; integrated enterprise strategies that ensure technology is ready when needed, competitively protected, and environmentally progressive; and disciplined and efficient engineering, operations, and supplier management support that ensures program success.

About the Guest Authors

Nihad Aytaman is Director of Business Applications at Elie Tahari (*www.elietahari.com*).

Jeff Guevin is Manager of BI Architecture at Martin's Point Health Care (*www.martinspoint.org*).

Mark Lack is Manager, Strategy Analytics and Business Intelligence, at Mueller, Inc. (*www.muellerinc.com*).

Thomas J. Marks is Continuous Improvement Process Manager at Daimler Trucks North America LLC (*www.daimler-trucksnorth america.com*).

Roland Mosimann is Chief Executive Officer at AlignAlytics (*www.alignalytics.com*).

Eric Place is Manager of BI Reporting and Analysis at Martin's Point Health Care (*www.martinspoint.org*).

Larry Yarter is Chief Architect, Business Analytics Center of Competence at IBM (*www.ibm.com*).

Contents

Introduction – The Business Analytics Program and Keys to Success 1

    The Business Analytics Program: Agility and Change............................. 3

    Business Analytics Maturity 4

    The Business Analytics Program 7

Chapter 1 – Key #1: Strategy..**11**

    The Strategy Framework 13

    Maturity of a Business Analytics Program Strategy............................... 15

    Risks of Strategy Fragmentation 19

    Strategy Alignment 20

    Maturing the Program with Business Domain Architectures 21

    Getting Started: Assessment of Strategy.. 23

    Creating the Kickoff Point.. 26

    Prioritization and Roadmap 27

    Metrics Framework and Measurement 28

    Managing a Changing Strategy 29

    Case Study on Strategy: Mueller, Inc. 31

    Strategy: Practical Tips for Identifying, Assessing, and Prioritizing Metrics........... 35

    Strategy Checklist... 46

Chapter 2 – Key #2: Value..**47**

    Describing Value: The Business Value Hierarchy 48

    Step 1: Building a Business Case 54

    Step 2: Building the Value Portfolio... 55

    Step 3: Business Analytics Metrics and Feedback 56

    Filling the Value Void 57

    Case Study on Value: IBM.. 60

    Practical Tips for Measuring and Demonstrating Value:

        Creating the Business Value Portfolio 63

    Value Checklist 64

Chapter 3 – Key #3: People **65**

Maturity of the Business Analytics Program 66

Executive Involvement 70

Organizational Design: The Business Analytics Center of Excellence 73

Skills, Talents, and Roles 76

Offshore or Outsource? 79

How Many Team Members Should Be in a Center of Excellence? 80

Relationship Management, Communication, and Evangelism 81

People: Success or Derailment 86

Case Study on People: Martin's Point Health Care 87

Practical Tips for Organizing People:

    Designing an Analytics Center of Excellence 92

People Checklist 96

Chapter 4 – Key #4: Process **97**

Maturity of the Business Analytics Program 98

Stakeholder Identification and New Project Start 99

Communication, Education, and Adoption 100

Proven Practice Sharing 101

Developing an Advise and Consult Framework 102

Streamlining Requirements Gathering 103

Agility in Development 104

Governance 105

Processes for Technology, Standards, and Innovation 109

Business Analytics Process Design 114

An Agile Business Analytics Process 115

Case Study on Process: Daimler Trucks North America 117

Practical Tips: How to Keep Business Analytics Processes Agile 121

Process Checklist 124

Chapter 5 – Key #5: Technology **125**

    Understanding Business Analytics Technology Maturity 127

    To Standardize or Not to Standardize? 127

    To Build or Buy? 128

    Evolving a BA Technology Strategy 129

    Business Strategy Requirements Evolution 130

    Architecting for User Adoption and Growth 133

    Deployment Approaches 135

    Innovation 137

    Technology Growth and Maturity 138

    Self-Service Impacts with Technology 139

    Converging Capabilities and Technology 140

    Case Study on Technology: Elie Tahari 142

    Practical Tips: Selecting Technologies for Your Business Analytics Needs 147

    Technology Checklist 149

Conclusion **151**

Preface

5 Keys to Business Analytics Program Success is an amalgamation of the combined experience of the members of the IBM Business Analytics Excellence Advisory Board. Our team has been documenting and sharing best practices since 2008, and this book builds on our first book, *Business Intelligence Strategy*, expanding our knowledge with additional sharing and viewpoints from five other companies with deep experience and proven excellence in Business Analytics.

This book is meant to be shared with aspiring business analytics program managers, senior executives, and IT or BA managers who are also trying to manage a program amidst an era of rapid technology evolution. If you are looking for a guide that will help you learn the features and functions of how to use Business Analytics technology, this book will not help you—this book is meant to discuss the management aspects of the program, as well as a bit of the sociology behind making it work.

It can be pointed out that the first book from this team contained the term "Business Intelligence" in the title, while the second discusses "Business Analytics." Both books actually discuss similar capabilities, but the change in terminology demonstrates the rapidly evolving landscape of Business Analytics. Just a couple years ago, Business Intelligence dominated the analytic landscape, encompassing and integrating with a variety of technologies. Today, the analytics landscape is so vast that the terms of reference themselves have changed.

So, what do we mean by Business Analytics? When we discuss Business Analytics (BA), we refer to the groups of analytical capabilities that are used to help organizations make better decisions. This includes Business Intelligence (reporting, analysis, scorecard, and dashboard capabilities), Performance Management (budgeting, planning, forecasting, and what-if scenario analysis), Predictive and Advanced Analytics (predictive and statistical analysis), as well as risk management solutions. While information management solutions—such as data warehousing, ETL (extract, transfer, load), data quality, and others—are the foundation of analytics and critical to the conversation, the focus of this book is less on this area of analytics, and we maintain most of the discussion at the analytic capability level.

This book is not just about implementing Business Analytics technologies; it's about *smarter* analytics. The goal is to achieve business outcomes—with decision making and the end result as the aim. It's about innovating and integrating technologies to produce the best results in the most efficient ways. It's about continually trying to move the marker to achieve higher levels of performance, of analytic maturity, and to constantly strive for excellence. Business Analytics is a technology that affects businesses on the front lines— and the management of business, governments, teams, and individuals. It produces real results and has the ability to deliver major impact.

However, the technologies are evolving rapidly, and keeping up with the change of pace is difficult. It must be recognized that it is a journey, not a destination. It's a program—not a project. This is why this book talks to the Program—not just the specific organizational design or the technology—but the overall program that will pervade the entire organization with analytic culture at its roots.

For many months, the team discussed the content that went into the book to help organizations understand the common practices that are followed by organizations—in any industry and of various sizes. All the while, we knew that the goal was to define the areas of focus for a Business Analytics Program, but we decided to hold the title until the end of the book. When the content was done, we had many debates about the name of the book. We knew there were five major areas of the Business Analytics Program—but were they five separate areas that needed to be managed separately and it didn't matter which came first? Or were they five different steps that should be followed one after the other? Were they rules? For many weeks, we discussed this topic and finally decided on "5 Keys" as the core concept of the title. We chose this title because each of the teams actually implemented the five areas at separate times and in different orders and still managed a very successful program. What we decided was that a business analytics program could successfully be implemented in any order—or parts of each area together at the same time—and create success. However, at the end we decided that if you actually implement the 5 Keys in the order we have stated in the book, your time to success will likely be more rapid. This is because if you have a strategy and attach value, it is much easier to design your organization, combat politics, design processes, and determine technology requirements. So, while any order will do, organizations new to analytics may wish to actually follow the order that is discussed in this book.

What we did realize is that there is really no one-size-fits-all program structure, organizational design, process, or technology architecture. It all depends on analytic maturity, culture, and need within each organization. However, there are common elements that each organization can take and adapt to its own environment. This book is not an academic overview, nor is it meant to be a prescriptive recipe—it is a practical guide of knowledge that can be adapted to meet the needs of any business.

This book is about collaborating, communicating, and creating change in an organization. It is about building knowledge, aligning an organization, being able to anticipate and shape outcomes, acting on knowledge, learning with every step, and transforming an organization. This is the recipe that creates smarter analytics.

Another interesting point to note is that the members of the author team come from various industries—manufacturing, life sciences, insurance, services, retail, and software—and regardless of the industry, each of our organizations has the same common program elements. No matter where you come from, the principles of running a successful Business Analytics Program are the very same.

We enjoyed the debates, discussions, and sharing that went into the creation of this book—and hope that the insight and best practices provide real learning to you in your Business Analytics journey. If you see the commonalities in your organization, then you can recognize that you are well on the path to a successful program—and you will see that the downfalls and the successes you encounter along this journey are normal. We hope you walk away with some new ideas and that you breathe a sigh of relief as you see some of your own struggles iterated in this book—hopefully with a solution you can implement that will help you to overcome your challenge. We appreciate any thoughts, feedback, or ideas you have—connect with any of us on LinkedIn to share your stories.

—John, Bill, Brian, Tracy, and Kay
October 2012

Introduction

The Business Analytics Program and Keys to Success

Business Analytics has evolved rapidly over the past few years and continues to be a top priority for organizations. It has risen out of the specialties of the information technology teams into the lines of business and all the way to the top of the organization's agenda. In the 2012 IBM CEO Study, 73 percent of CEOs indicated that they were making significant investments in their organizations' ability to draw meaningful customer insights from available data[1]. As a mission-critical system, the CEO now expects analytics to provide information at the fingertips of the teams that run the business.

In our first book, *Business Intelligence Strategy: A Practical Guide for Achieving BI Excellence*[2], we examined how to create an all-inclusive strategy to ensure a Business Intelligence (BI) and Business Analytics (BA) initiative could get off to a healthy start. Having a clear strategy and vision is a critical factor that impacts the ability of an organization to achieve success in a strategic Business Analytics initiative. We emphasized that success is based on the overall business strategy, which must address the future vision for technology, people (culture and organization), and process. The strategy should create a roadmap for how the organization will move forward in a series of measurable successes rather than using a "big bang" approach.

However, strategy alone will not ensure success; *executing* on this strategy is often where challenges arise. When we look back, an article from *Fortune* magazine more than 10 years ago, entitled "Why CEOs Fail," estimated that fewer than 10 percent of companies were successfully executing on the critical strategies the CEOs had identified for their organizations:

> "The problem is that our age's fascination with strategy and vision feeds the mistaken belief that developing exactly the right strategy will enable a company to rocket past competitors. In reality, that's less than half the battle."[3]

Developing the capability to actually *execute* on a winning strategy is the missing half of the equation. Although an organization may have a compelling strategy, it is often challenged in its inability to translate business strategy into actionable plans of achievement.

---

[1] "Leading Through Connections: Insights from the Global IBM CEO Study." IBM, Institute for Business Value, May 2012.

[2] John Boyer, Bill Frank, Brian Green, Tracy Harris, and Kay Van De Vanter. *Business Intelligence Strategy: A Practical Guide for Achieving BI Excellence.* Ketchum, ID: MC Press, 2010.

[3] R. Charan and G. Colvin. "Why CEOs Fail," *Fortune*, June 21, 1999.

Today, the number of organizations now linking strategy to execution has tripled to 30 percent[4]—a number that is promising. How has this jump occurred? What are these organizations now doing differently from the other 70 percent? We believe that one factor is the advances that have occurred in technology. Technology is an enabler. Technology can enable companies to process more data, more quickly than ever before. We cannot assume, however, that simply because we can produce reports faster we are adding value. It is only when the technology strategy is linked to the four other "Keys to Business Analytics Program Success" that we can really demonstrate value. In other words, it is not solely the advancement of technology that has contributed to more organizations linking strategy to execution; it is that these organizations have recognized how to leverage that technology. They have learned the benefit of demonstrating value by leveraging technology to support or enable people and processes and ultimately supporting the organizational strategy. So, it may be that because technology is more of an enabler and can support the ability to execute on strategy, it has more pervasive dependencies on the other keys we discuss.

A recent IBM Institute for Business Value study[5] discovered that organizations that use *analytics* outperform their peers by 2.2 times. It appears that a major factor in being able to achieve high performance lies in the ability to seize the advances in the analytic technologies that are available. These new technologies help executives, managers, and employees better monitor their business, plan collaboratively among various stakeholders, and integrate diverse sets of data to be transformed into knowledge.

> A recent IBM CFO study shows that Chief Financial Officers in organizations that make extensive use of analytics report growth in revenues of 36 percent or more, a 15 percent greater return on invested capital and twice the rate of growth in EBITDA (earnings before interest, taxes, depreciation and amortization).[6]

However, many organizations are still in early stages of using analytic technologies effectively. In fact, the same statistic that looks so promising also shows that many organizations still are not linking their stated strategy to their execution of this strategy.

That is because, as mentioned, neither a spectacular strategy nor advanced technologies in isolation will achieve success; they are each important elements but do not stand alone—similar to legs on a stool. A strategy is required to plan, set targets, and goals. The strategy gives legs to the vision and what is expected. Technologies can support an organization to do things faster, quicker, easier, or with more precision—but to collectively understand the expectations and how an organization is going to get there and execute effectively requires yet another set of skills and the creation of a program that will tie the two together.

---

[4] Analytics Quotient Study. IBM, 2012.

[5] "Breaking Away with Business Analytics and Optimization." IBM Institute for Business Value, 2009.

[6] 2009 research based on "The New Value Integrator: Insights from the Global Chief Financial Officer Study." IBM Institute for Business Value, 2010.

The Business Analytics Program: Agility and Change

So, you have now crafted your strategy—what next? You need to put your Business Analytics Program in place. As you might expect, each of our organizations has gone through a number of evolutionary steps to reach their current operational levels of maturity. Each of our organizations has taken a different path. Let's clearly state today that there is no single "silver bullet" when it comes to running a Business Analytics Program—no single program methodology—and the strategy, organization, and technology you put in place today will change as your organization matures in its ability to use analytic technologies. You need to expect this, embrace it, and change with it. This is why it is called a *program*—and not a project. It is a collection or succession of projects. We also believe this is why the term "Agile BI" is so popular today. Agility and change are really what a successful Program is about.

- **A Business Analytics Program is:**
  - How you implement the strategy, people, processes, and technologies to achieve business outcomes
  - Able to address innovation, transformation, standardization, and other dynamic factors
  - A fluid, changing, agile set of teams, processes, and projects
  - A long-term series of activities, plans, procedures, and projects managed by a team characterized by both virtual and structured relationships

- **A Business Analytics Program is not:**
  - A single office and organizational structure
  - A temporary construct to solve an immediate need
  - A set of processes and policies that are rigid and unable to change or adapt
  - A single technology to which teams must adhere

You will notice we specifically point out that a Business Analytics Program is not an organizational structure. This book will discuss the organizational construct that leads and governs the Program—the Analytics Center of Excellence—but this construct is but one component of a Business Analytics Program. While the Analytics Center of Excellence is a key driver of the program, the program itself will have people, processes, and technologies that stretch outside the visible analytics teams.

A Business Analytics Program is largely designed to manage change over the long term—and this change will occur as the Business Analytics initiative matures. The structure and organizational chart will change over time and with maturity, as will the processes, policies, and technologies that are used. In each of the sections we will discuss in this book, you will see us address the question of how to remain agile as the program grows, as well as the importance of agility in the Business Analytics Program.

Business Analytics Maturity

A Business Analytics Program does not develop overnight; it matures over time. The elements that make up the Program will change over time as the Program matures, and program managers need to recognize change and nurture it to achieve the highest levels of maturity.

Over the years, a number of different maturity models have been developed to describe the Business Analytics journey and the readiness of an enterprise to synthesize and organize its Business Analytics infrastructure. Some of these have been devised by academics and others by analysts or technology vendors. These models are descriptive tools that help organizations identify where they reside on a spectrum of Business Analytics implementation. All of the models build a hierarchy of steps, from the most basic implementation of Business Intelligence or reporting through more advanced, coordinated implementations and infrastructures.

As we evaluated our Business Analytics processes during the development of our first book, we quickly realized that the separate paths taken by our enterprises—and our individual teams—still had many common threads. These paths led each organization past very recognizable milestones, and we've seen how these milestones describe the evolutionary steps *every* organization experiences in its Business Analytics development.

It doesn't matter whether your organization is large or small—the same concepts still apply, though each has its individual challenges. Whereas smaller organizations may have fewer resources to rely on in terms of budget or talent, larger organizations also have their difficulties with larger networks of employees and rationalization of individual departmental strategies. At the heart of the matter, recognizing that key elements of people, process, and technologies are required for success and that a concerted effort needs to be made to bring the alignment across the organization is where you will find that success can be achieved.

By examining the characteristics of these milestones, your organization can better understand the challenges (and the opportunities) that lie ahead on your path toward Business Analytics excellence. This exercise is helpful in designing a Business Analytics Program that will support the organization over the long term—and allow you to recognize the various stages and changes that will need to be addressed. You can measure these steps in a variety of ways, but as an example, we will review IBM's **Analytics Quotient (AQ) Maturity Model**[7].

Like the IQ tests that were developed to measure the intelligence of individuals, IBM has developed an AQ test to measure analytic maturity in an organization. AQ measures how ready you are to apply insight to your strategy, processes, and tactics; how quickly you can reallocate resources and reorient your people to make better decisions; and how

7 Analytics Quotient website (*http://www.ibm.com/software/analytics/aq*). IBM, 2012.

effectively you can act based on how well you know your past performance, current results, and future possibilities.

What's Your AQ?

The AQ concept has two core components. The first component assesses the organization's decision-making power and its use of analytics, as well as the culture that surrounds it. Examples of areas examined include:

- What is the quality of the information you use to make decisions?
- How do you measure that quality?
- What is your strategy for leveraging analytics?
- Have you documented successful outcomes of analytics initiatives in your organization?
- What percentage of your decision makers uses analytics to inform and make decisions?
- How do you anticipate future events and results?

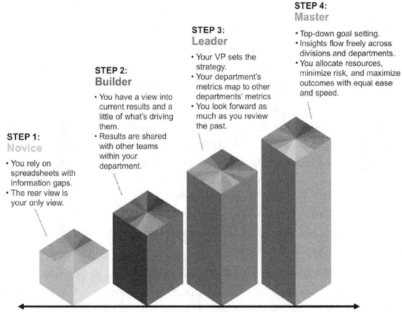

STEP 1:
Novice
- You rely on spreadsheets with information gaps.
- The rear view is your only view.

STEP 2:
Builder
- You have a view into current results and a little of what's driving them.
- Results are shared with other teams within your department.

STEP 3:
Leader
- Your VP sets the strategy.
- Your department's metrics map to other departments' metrics
- You look forward as much as you review the past.

STEP 4:
Master
- Top-down goal setting.
- Insights flow freely across divisions and departments.
- You allocate resources, minimize risk, and maximize outcomes with equal ease and speed.

Manual, slow, error prone, cumbersome, fragmented
Data quality concerns

Automated, instant, accurate, seamless, converged
Data governance is in place

Figure 1: Analytics Quotient (AQ) Maturity Model

The second component of the AQ Maturity Model maps the numerical score in the first component to one of four stages of increasing analytical maturity (Figure 1). Again, like IQ, the higher you are on the scale, the better your organization is likely to perform.

The AQ Maturity Model looks at various elements that derive from strategy, organizational and cultural behavior, as well as the technologies used in the organization.

After completing the *academic* exercise of assessing the AQ of an enterprise, there are practical benefits in understanding where your organization fits into the spectrum of analytics sophistication.

First of all, larger organizations are the first to recognize that different areas/silos within the enterprise will probably exist at different levels of analytic sophistication. For instance, the AQ of a particular department or subsidiary may be at a significantly lower level of sophistication than that of another department or subsidiary.

This is not necessarily a negative state of affairs, but a natural result of how analytics is moving and being adapted through the organization. Yet, by mapping those areas using the AQ Maturity Model, the organization can identify where assigning more resources may deliver greater value as a whole. Once AQ has been assessed, the Business Analytics Program can use this maturity rating to further assist those sectors of the organization, to raise their AQ to deliver better, more consistent analytics to the benefit of the business strategy and the success of the organization as a whole.

Second, as the organization changes its business strategy over time, the Business Analytics Program can better target those areas with specific suggestions—including added technology and training—to help those areas better succeed.

Finally, as the organization progresses through the various maturity levels of Novice, Builder, and Leader toward mastery, the ability of the organization to respond to new strategic challenges grows as well. The AQ Maturity Model demonstrates, first, how the program must keep agile and changing. The goal is not to have a monolithic technology infrastructure but an *open and collaborative* structure that is capable of adapting to new requirements. Assessing the AQ of an organization enables management and teams to see new opportunities. These new opportunities are derived from understanding the diverse analytic silos and then assisting them to grow and mature in a way that will deliver success for the organization overall.

Organizations will also go beyond Business Analytics Program agility to experience value in performance outcomes. By nurturing the capabilities of Business Analytics within the enterprise, we have seen our organizations grow in robust information resources that support the decision makers in their daily tasks. This results in IT efficiency, business efficiency, and business effectiveness and transformation of the organization by moving from strategy through to execution.

By now, you may have a Business Analytics Strategy in hand—you have a vision, and you have informally begun collaborating with business champions in the organization to define your goals. You have a vision of how the strategy will be implemented, and you've assessed your organization against the AQ Maturity Model—now where to start? It's time to put the formal Business Analytics Program in place and get moving!

The Business Analytics Program

Many organizations overestimate the ease by which a formal Business Analytics Program is put in place. They may not recognize the breadth of impact the program will have on the organization. It is often believed that the hard decisions are over once you choose a technology. The technology in itself has been identified at times as the easier part of the equation. It's the people, processes, and culture of the organization that can often present continual challenges.

Like the strategy that goes before it, the Business Analytics Program needs to constantly maintain and adapt its various components. A few analytic experts sitting in a line-of-business (LOB) department using a flashy new tool don't equate to a successful Business Analytics Program. Nor does an IT team with a data warehouse. Quite the contrary. A Business Analytics Program singlehandedly run by a few members of an IT team is likely to experience many political roadblocks. While a program has to start somewhere, it is also premature for an organization just dipping its toes into analytic technologies to explain to the executive team a vision of a complex Business Analytics Program with cross-departmental collaboration, and dedicated resources with technology standards, without internal proof points on how it has made an initial difference. This is why a vision that includes change and maturity over time is necessary.

Figure 2: 5 Keys to a Successful Business Analytics Program

In the next several chapters, we discuss the five essential elements—or *keys*—that we believe need make up a successful Business Analytics Program (Figure 2). And we share some practical advice you can start using today as you create a program that is right for your organization's maturity and culture.

These essential elements include:

1. **Strategy:** Creating a strategy once doesn't mean you have completed the task. A strategy will change over time, and it requires ongoing focus and attention. While strategy is the driving force of a Business Analytics Program, it often can be undefined in terms of ownership. The importance of this element of the initiative merits increased focus because there is rarely a central coordinating body and the initiative may consist of many owners. In the Strategy chapter (Chapter 1), we discuss practical examples of core elements of managing a changing strategy, such as:

    *   Stakeholder assessment and identification
    *   Assessment of strategy
    *   Business alignment
    *   Prioritization and roadmap
    *   Metrics framework and measurement
    *   Strategy development and change

2. **Value:** Understanding and documenting the success and business cases will increase the value of the overall Business Analytics Program; however, this is often the first area to suffer neglect when the team is busy with the day-to-day tactics. Building a value portfolio, defining outcomes and targets, and measuring success often falls behind other priorities—causing difficulty when teams want to go back for additional resource investment. In the Value chapter (Chapter 2), we discuss:

    *   Business case
    *   Value portfolio—including IT efficiency, business efficiency, and business effectiveness
    *   BI metrics and feedback

3. **People:** A Business Analytics Program involves a wide range of people throughout the organization, and ensuring the right ones are on board and having an organization to support this will increase your success. We agree that the people element of the program is where you will face risk of derailment if this element is not managed well. In the People chapter (Chapter 3), we discuss a few areas of focus that will increase your success and discuss some of the challenges you can avoid, including:

    *   Organizational design—the Analytics Center of Excellence
    *   Skills, talent, and roles
    *   Relationship management, communication, and evangelism
    *   Executive management support

4. **Process:** A Business Analytics Program needs to implement processes, policies, and guidelines that will help assist the team's success. However, it can easily become bogged down with process—and agility will suffer. Process needs to be implemented, monitored, and continually evaluated to ensure you can grow yet maintain an Agile Business Analytics Program. In the Process chapter (Chapter 4), we discuss:

   - License and standards management
   - Support
   - Education and adoption
   - Requirements gathering
   - Governance—strategy, data, change, IT, and platforms
   - Process design
   - Proven practice sharing
   - Advise and consult framework

5. **Technology:** Technology is, of course, the backbone of the entire program—but technology should follow and not lead the program. Understanding the business need behind the technology implementation—and the technology selection—is required to ensure the technology can meet the needs of the business. At the same time, because innovation is rapid today, users may not know the "art of the possible." A balance between the two must be recognized. In the Technology chapter (Chapter 5), we discuss:

   - Choosing capabilities that fit the business needs
   - Introducing a platform of standards
   - Information Management and governance
   - Encouraging adoption with the right architecture, performance, and scalability
   - Continual innovation

Across each of our organizations, these five key areas were consistently identified as elements that require focus in order to increase the success of a Business Analytics Program. Each of our organizations matured in these areas as our Business Analytics Programs grew, most often beginning as a fairly small group of like-minded analytic champions—in some cases virtual with a common vision, working together—and gradually putting in processes to develop a robust multi-discipline program that crossed departments and gained momentum over time.

This is why program maturity is central to this book—each of our organizations went through it, and we discovered that there were several things we did in common that helped our organizations succeed:

✓ **Small steps:** Taking small steps, instead of "boiling the ocean," and creating a series of successes that continually drove trust and interest in the program

✓ **Communication and collaboration:** Open communication and collaboration to drive far-reaching teams together in a vision

✓ **Agility and openness:** Remaining agile and open to change, and discussing and debating needs and requirements

✓ **Self-service:** Ensuring self-service and access instead of being gatekeepers to information or holding up business requirements

In the following chapters, we share our view of these elements that we believe are the most critical components you need to consider for your program as you rise through the maturity levels—with a goal to help others create a successful Business Analytics Program on their own. Each organization is different—and may manage these elements differently—but they are a group of elements that need to be considered throughout the lifecycle of your Business Analytics Program.

Chapter 1
Key #1: Strategy

The first key to a successful Business Analytics Program that we will discuss is the strategy. In a Business Analytics Program, we mentioned that one of the most critical, yet commonly overlooked, essential elements of focus is around the changing strategy. Not only does an initial vision need to be developed for an organization, but a way to review the strategy, the changing needs throughout the organization, and the program processes developed along the way is also necessary as an ongoing and core element of the program.

Many organizations begin analytic initiatives with grassroots efforts—and sometimes it may not be the lack of strategy but rather too many silos of strategy that create the initial difficulty in managing the program. As an organization matures in its analytic capability or Business Analytics technologies, it often later surfaces that a cohesive strategy is required to increase collaboration and decision making, reduce costs, and steer the ship in the same direction to achieve corporate goals.

It is also one of the top reasons a Business Analytics Program often doesn't show expected value. Without defined direction, goals, outcomes, and a way to execute that is a shared vision with the key stakeholders, siloed initiatives occur that produce only small, tactical, and incremental gains. It is often a process of analytic maturity that helps organizations realize the opportunities and gains that can be made by strategically planning their Business Analytics programs in their organizations.

Our organizations were among the various pioneers of the early Business Intelligence Programs that evolved to Business Analytics. We experienced growing pains throughout the process, but we blazed a trail to analytic maturity where we can share practical tips for moving a program at a more rapid pace. How quickly you rise beyond the silos of analytics into a more collaborative approach can depend on how the program is managed—but the pressures of a constantly changing environment always need to be recognized and continually planned for. We will identify some key forward-looking elements that will help you shortcut some common challenges.

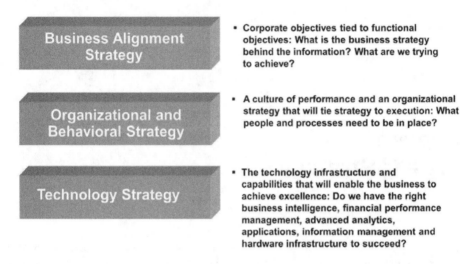

Figure 3: Strategy Framework[1]

It doesn't mean that silo deployments aren't valuable as a starting point, or as a way to realize value. Quite the contrary: Analytics silos are often a starting point to short-term tactical gains that develop the appetite—and provide an initial training ground—for more strategic analytics. However, the longer-term benefits are frequently driven by cross-functional collaboration—which can often take more time and require more planning due to the politics and complexity of the task. Therefore, we recommend putting a program in place that supports the people, process, and technology elements that will deliver the long-term benefits as a highly successful best practice.

A successful Business Analytics Program starts with a well-defined, coordinated business and IT strategy. This will require a continual focus on the strategy itself and constant adjustments to ensure the organization understands the goals and expected outcomes, prioritizes, and connects the analytics strategy to the corporate strategy. The strategy should have both a long-term vision and a pragmatic series of steps and a roadmap on how you plan to get there. It should also address the many factors at play—factors that move beyond the technology itself and encompass the people, processes, and business drivers that create the need for a Business Analytics Program. Most important, it will recognize that it will change over time.

---

[1] John Boyer, Bill Frank, Brian Green, Tracy Harris, and Kay Van De Vanter. *Business Intelligence Strategy: A Practical Guide for Achieving BI Excellence."* Ketchum, ID: MC Press, 2010.

The Strategy Framework

In our first book, we introduced what we called the "Strategy Framework." This framework consists of three distinct parts (depicted in Figure 3):

- **A business alignment strategy:** Understanding the overall business strategy and then tying corporate objectives to functional objectives so that the application of the Business Analytics Strategy is of high value, understood, and aligned. Identifying what the business strategy is behind the information is absolutely the most critical step in the strategy. Technologies are not implemented for the sake of technology—there are business goals that teams need
- to be working toward to realize value.
- **An organizational and behavioral strategy:** Creating the right culture that drives performance and an organizational strategy that will tie business strategy to execution. This is the glue that will help the people in the organization clearly realize the use of technology and modify behaviors that will ensure the right processes are implemented and a data-driven culture can be embraced.
- **A technology strategy:** Identifying the technology infrastructure and capabilities that will enable the business to achieve excellence: Do we have the right capabilities for the right individuals to be able to monitor, analyze, predict, and develop a plan of action to support the strategy? How are we implementing these technologies to ensure we are achieving the lowest total cost of ownership (TCO) while enabling the business to be successful? How are we including newer innovation, whether it's mobile strategy, big data, self-service, cloud, or other technologies?

Under each of these aspects, several areas need to be addressed and considered when preparing a strategy. The Strategy Framework is a practical guide that organizations in any industry can use to help create a strategy. It is the foundation for creating the Business Analytics Program.

However, there are times when creation of the Business Analytics Strategy has also run awry—when teams prepare a strategy in a silo without consulting the broader organizational stakeholders that need to embrace the strategy. These deviations may occur intentionally or unintentionally—unintentionally when teams attempt to boil the ocean, or intentionally when they become too focused on technology, risking loss of confidence and support of critical key stakeholders. So let's take a moment to look at what a strategy should and should not be:

- **A Business Analytics Strategy *is not*:**
  - A single destination or one-time project
  - A siloed effort of one department (it may start in one area, and there may be tactical strategies in that department, but it should not remain a siloed initiative if analytic maturity is the goal)

- ○ A requirements document for reports or a dashboard
- ○ Just about information technology and the IT department (e.g., a document the IT team prepares about technology selection)
- ○ A 400-page document that is circulated to all the teams
- ○ An architecture design or vision

- **A Business Analytics Strategy *is*:**

  - ○ A roadmap that demonstrates and includes a long-term vision, created as a roadmap of smaller wins and iterations supported by key stakeholders that supports business strategies (e.g., gaining market share, increasing revenues, reducing costs, discovering opportunities)
  - ○ A collaborative effort across teams—line of business, finance, IT—that takes people, process, and technology into consideration
  - ○ A journey that is fluid, changing, and agile and requires commitments of people, funding, and governance
  - ○ A series of documents agreed, communicated, committed to, and embraced by a particular audience at a particular point in time

Implementing a Business Intelligence technology is <u>not</u> a Business Analytics Strategy. It is but one tactic of many that will help facilitate the end goal.

Tactics will help an organization achieve the larger corporate or organizational strategic goals, such as lowering operational costs, increasing market penetration, and/or achieving better returns on investment for shareholders. However tactics, in and of themselves, don't rise to the level of strategies.

Tactical Conflicts

When a tactic is implemented as a strategy, confusion rises among the masses. The tactics of one department, subsidiary, or silo may actually result in conflict with the tactics of another entity, further confusing management's alignment with the overall business strategy. A strategy needs to be supported by objectives, and tactics should definitely support the overall plan—but it is easy for organizations to jump to tactics to try to solve a problem quickly.

For instance, multiple Business Analytics Programs within a company may develop conflicting data and reports, making it more difficult for information users to get a clear perspective on progress toward strategic or tactical goals. Trying to rectify the problem by implementing a common technology platform may not, and likely will not, solve the problem if the information that is being presented is different or subject to interpretation (e.g., lack of consistent master data, dimensional conformity, metadata).

This presents a delicate conundrum: How can an organization execute on its strategy in an environment in which a wide variety of conflicting tactical tools are used across multiple information silos?

There should be a clear overall business strategy as a first step. All companies develop short- and long-term business plans. The Business Analytics Strategy should then support these plans—managing the processes required to bring the intelligence (via the information value chain) together. Companies then need to bring the IT, line-of-business, and various other teams together to develop insights and drive action that stems from these insights to move forward. This step is as critical as the strategy itself in a successful organization. Harnessing the technology that can better inform and enable these teams forward is a necessary task. Technology is the relatively easy part, however, only if these other components of the Business Analytics Strategy are in place.

This framework provides a practical guide to help an organization understand many of the considerations it needs to include in a strategy. What it will not do is provide you with a "cookie-cutter" strategy. It recognizes that each organization is different; culture, structure, maturity level, and strategy will all affect a Business Analytics Program, and each of these needs to be part of the well-thought-out plan to ensure success.

Just as a Business Analytics Program is a journey, so is the strategy—an ongoing effort that should, in fact, change over time, should be measured regularly against established benchmarks, and should be flexible enough to change. It should also be reviewed, adjusted, and agreed to on a regular basis and tweaked and realigned to ensure it is meeting the evolving expectations of the business.

In this chapter, we provide specific practical tips that will help you create and manage your Business Analytics Program strategy to ensure it takes into account the various areas of strategy and allows for change, maturity, and growth. We discuss:

- Maturity of a Business Analytics Program strategy
- Assessment of strategy
- Strategy design
- Business strategy alignment
- Prioritization and roadmap
- Metrics framework and measurement
- Managing ongoing strategy change

By understanding these areas and proactively building a strategy that will support a growing Business Analytics Program over time, organizations will benefit with a more rapid road to success and the ability to achieve performance goals.

Maturity of a Business Analytics Program Strategy

To help understand the journey of what strategy evolution looks like over time for a Business Analytics Program, we will use the concept of the Analytics Quotient Maturity Model that demonstrates the journey over time. While each journey often has many evolutions, there are common patterns that we have seen regardless of our industry or organizational makeup. By understanding some of these common evolutions and charting a typical journey, we feel it will help an organization identify the current state of its Business Analytics Program and outline a path to build its vision.

If we look back to the early stages, before a formal Business Analytics Program was officially kicked off, a Business Analytics Strategy may not have formally existed within the organization. There is likely always a corporate business strategy, but it may be supported by a variety of disconnected analytics strategies on how to achieve those goals—each monitoring the business the best way it knows how. A variety of tools and varying levels of skilled individuals that can use analytic tools and data management strategies exist in the various business areas. Without a defined Business Analytics Strategy, there is potential for disconnect between business units, technology strategies, and information silos.

It is often not the lack of business strategy that creates a challenge, but rather the instance of too many silos of strategy evolving from the core framework that creates chaos. Without a coordination beyond the top-level strategy, it creates an organization and infrastructure where information likely resides in various pockets within the organization, but there's no clear consensus between both business and IT to bring that information into a form that is useful to support the business strategy. Individuals get used to running heroics to pull data when asked and spend time on spreadsheets and various tools to answer business questions in a reactive fashion. This may create local heroes, but it is not optimal for the enterprise and may actually be detrimental. IT teams understand that there is a data challenge, but they may not understand the priorities or have the support of the business to manage the data.

The early stages of analytics in an organization may be perpetuated for a considerable period of time as the different entities within the organization struggle to meet continual information demands and as the enterprise fails to understand the benefits of data integration and the accompanying analytics that are enabled via a coordinated Business Analytics Strategy. In fact, quite often these various entities don't completely understand the overall strategy but are only responding to the requests for unique pieces of information. As time goes on, each siloed entity may have developed its own techniques for defining goals and accumulating data, forming its own automation strategy to make that data available. This includes using a variety of spreadsheets, databases, dashboards, and other analytic tools and analysis methods.

> "In our recent AQ study[2], 45 percent of participants indicated their analytics strategy was very fragmented or departmentally based rather than strategic with executive-level focus. A great way to accelerate strategy and success in an early-stage program is to create the open dialogue across teams and between stakeholders that can directly influence a

---

[2] Analytics Quotient Study. IBM, 2012.

> change, whether they are in the business, finance, or IT. Learn where
> strategy originates and how each team copes with strategy change.
> Understand top-level business priorities so you can determine who
> your key stakeholders should be. Find out how often formal business
> strategy is reviewed, what the process is, and what tools they are using.
> Communication and understanding current state is key."
>
> —*Tracy Harris, Senior Manager, Business Analytics Excellence, IBM*

Yet, the longer organizations take a tactical approach to respond to business challenges without a clear image of how the information can be used by senior management and across teams and business domains, the greater the danger of redundancy, the potential for misinformation, and, in the worst case, the chance of failure to comply with regulations or internal company rules. Plus, the more diverse the implementations of tools, the more difficult it is to pull together accurate or consistent information across the enterprise.

When these needs are recognized among a savvy team of champions, this is the time that the Business Analytics Program often begins to formulate. A group of stakeholders begins to identify the need to apply analytics with a consolidated set of data and reporting tools, apply structure to the various information requests, and consider the necessary metrics required to move into the next stage of the process. There may be a specific driver that is recognized as requiring cross-functional collaboration, such as trying to get a 360-degree view of the customer. Sometimes, a savvy executive or champion that has become versed in Business Analytics or who has seen success in the past from analytics initiatives that are cross-functionally oriented pulls the teams together. The Business Analytics Program is born, and communication across information domains begins to be realized. As the needs of the decision makers become clearer, departments or domains begin working together to understand how best to source and supply the supporting information. This working group typically focuses on a few top needs of the business where a few information areas can most logically come together. We call them sweet spots of information—the proposed outcomes and key areas that deliver value to the business strategy as identified by the group; the process is best managed by designing a roadmap detailing how to prioritize and then accumulate and organize the data for analysis. At this stage, the value of the sweet spots needs to be rated against the ease of creating and deploying solutions to achieve the desired results. The roadmap should be prioritized to facilitate a series of small successes to drive momentum for the project. Over time, following this skeletal roadmap, more sweet spots will be identified, prioritized, and achieved in the process. This step-by-step iterative process helps to eliminate initial frustrations, keeps the initial project on track, and builds support for the overall program through time. This process is also critical to staying agile over time, with teams working closely to achieve the project together.

However, a risk is that as successes build, the number of requests for reports, dashboards, scorecards, and analytical capabilities typically also grows exponentially, and the organization now discovers that it has trouble assimilating and supporting them all. At this stage, the program needs to undergo a change to remain agile. Decisions have to be made to empower teams, and high involvement from executive levels is needed to prioritize the resulting information and keep teams working together. In essence, they will be zeroing in and refining the definition of the identified sweet spots. The focus of the Business Analytics Program often changes from actually tactically doing the work to advising, consulting with, and empowering teams and coordinating the communications across the enterprise—the initial Business Analytics structure may evolve to a Business Analytics Strategy center.

As these priorities are established, the group further collaborates to target the areas, departments, and processes that will need to be put in place to reap the highest benefit and maintain agility. For its part, IT involvement might focus technically on the back end to identify how an infrastructure can be implemented. Meanwhile, business users begin to take responsibility for managing their own intelligence. At this point, strategy management to maintain a metrics framework will be critical; otherwise, the multiple reports with different definitions will create frustrations. Establishing a team to determine the appropriate definitions and recommend solutions will help the program maintain success.

Finally, as the program matures, the realization of change will occur once again. With a data-driven culture, competitive advantage occurs and more advanced analytics become the norm. Organizations are proactive rather than reactive, and analytics are embraced broadly by users across the business. The work is never done, however, as continual changes occur in the business, innovations are constantly on the horizon, and teams need to be able to remain agile to evaluate new technologies and integrate them into the portfolio. Sustaining the organization's enthusiasm in the overall program, remaining agile, and continuing to capture the trust of the users is an ongoing part of the Business Analytics Program.

The key to keeping on this path is to ensure there is a team that is wise to viewing the "big picture" of strategy to execution. Understanding how business strategy will impact the Business Analytics Strategy and how the program should start small and branch into new areas as successes accumulate is definitely a proven practice for success. Having a vision for the future and understanding the roadmap is key to executing successfully. By keeping the scope of the project within an achievable scale, the entire organization learns from the process, frustrations are minimized, and the business strategy is enhanced by a program that is robust, maintainable, and repeatable for future strategy initiatives.

Risks of Strategy Fragmentation

As straightforward as this maturity progression may appear on paper, there are serious risks. And the primary risk is the fragmentation of the initiatives for change.

> "Domains sprouting up like islands in the sea is a natural process. It's nature's way of trying to create order out of chaos on the small islands where we have control. The challenge is to manage it by providing an opportunity to collaborate and merge."
>
> —*John Boyer, Manager, Director, RCG Global Services*

For instance, there's a danger that the change in business strategy may spawn an actual increase in number of information repositories that may not share master, meta, or dimensional data, reducing the capability for cross-domain analytics. This most often occurs at the stage when the number of analytic demands hits—and begins to overwhelm the abilities of departments to manage them. The strategy must plan for this key stage to maintain agility—when the number of requests multiplies, the spawning of multiple Analytics Centers of Excellence within the various business units may create a lack of connection between them. Users may also decide to bypass the standard processes and procedures if they appear too time-consuming or difficult.

And while providing self-service and empowerment to the various teams is exactly the key to success, too many siloed and fixed structures can also degrade effectiveness with disconnected business strategies—and lower efficiencies with scattered and uncoordinated silos of information and limited sharing of best practices. The team that manages strategy needs to be aware of the signs of fragmentation and understand how the disconnect is occurring to open lines of communication and collaboration.

Another result caused by the spawning is the political conundrum: With too many centers—representing different segments of the business and each purporting to "speak" for its constituents and stakeholders—the culture of collaboration can deteriorate. Sometimes, at this juncture, the teams may see each other as competition with one another, creating further political complications, confusion, and ultimately long delays. This is where an Analytics Center of Excellence with a Strategy Center— which we will discuss in detail in Chapter 3—needs to play a key role in maintaining the strategy and creating the culture of communication. In many cases, companies employ a Chief Evangelist or Steering Committee concept, whose members are responsible for overseeing change and maintaining communication and collaboration. While we agree that the Strategy Center is very rare and present only in the most mature of organizations today, we believe that a formal group—and potentially an executive-level figure such as the "Chief Analytics Officer"—will become a must-have for organizations in the future to better manage this effort. This center and top executive could accelerate analytic strategy and performance of organizations.

Forward-Looking Statement

A Chief Analytics Officer and Strategy Center will become a driving force in organizations of the future.

So there is a delicate balance, with the overall goal of the process remaining at the top: building the agility of the organization to respond to current and future business strategy changes.

> "The risk of re-fragmentation is very real in a mature and competitive organization. While anything that challenges the norms and standards can be disruptive, it does help ensure that the organization continues to transform and grow. A key to dealing with this effectively is developing and communicating a clear set of roles for managing all aspects of Business Analytics: strategy, administration, training, data stewardship, governance, architecture, et cetera. A silo within an organization who may be 'shopping' for new capabilities is more likely to engage appropriately when the support roles are clearly understood."
>
> —*Brian Green, Manager, Business Intelligence & Performance Management, BlueCross BlueShield of Tennessee*

Strategy Alignment

The first question a Business Analytics Program manager needs to ask is how connected to the priorities of the business is the program overall today? Both inside the organization with linkages to top strategic objectives as well as outside the organization with partners, customers, or suppliers? How are you managing those connections? Is your program a central IT program that has low user adoption and business teams going off on their own with their disconnected analytic sandboxes? Or, perhaps, is your program one of those disconnected sandboxes that has little connection to what other teams are doing with your silo of data? It's likely both of these scenarios exist in your organization as it is quite common—and just a sign of an earlier maturity level that has yet to fully realize the benefits of a powerful Business Analytics Program. Either of these signs is positive, however, because it shows there is a thirst for knowledge and that there are champions in the business who can create change.

Where these IT, finance, or line-of-business teams need to meet is at a collaborative state with direct influence from the top down and across each of the business units. Ensuring that communication is flowing easily and that team members understand how directly their work ties to the strategies of the business is the goal. This does not mean a small team of people has to "do it all" across every unit of the business—it means there is strong empowerment across the business areas that know their business and there is a framework and communication vehicle in place to ensure trust and communication exist between them. It also means there is a direct link into strategy so that as the strategy changes, the program can proactively change with it. Without this ability to have a close connection between IT, business, and finance teams, agility will be lost and the value will never be fully realized. This will also become more important as the big data opportunity pushes the boundaries and opens the possibilities of exploring data outside the traditional systems of record. Trust, communication, and collaboration are key to ensuring that teams are working together cohesively; sharing insights, technology, and best practices; and targeting the most valuable areas of analytic insights.

Maturing the Program with Business Domain Architectures

Many of our Business Analytics Programs were fully realized when they were initially funded through executive mandate, based upon the value projects that were funded solely on their merits. These initial projects had proved the worth of a Business Analytics Program structure and demonstrated how its processes brought value to the organization. After centralizing the initiative to gain value and establish an information strategy, we were able to develop a common vision and direction for our analytics strategy. However, as more projects were initiated, establishing an architecture of business domain areas within the program was the most logical means of maintaining visibility and agility while sustaining control. We chose the word "domain" because analytic insight often crosses traditional department boundaries. For example, gaining a better view of the customer required collaboration of sales, marketing, operations, and finance. Each domain and department had a series of competing demands; therefore, this was the practice of creating a strategy whereby we could identify leaders and teams and interlock evangelists to support the competing demands while ensuring strong collaboration was central to the initiative. The key was to identify:

- Leaders who held the vision of the business strategy
- Business specialty professionals who could identify the requirements to meet the business demands
- Skilled analytic professionals who could map the needs to the data
- Technical professionals who could help to innovate with technology solutions
- Strategy managers who could ensure open communication, priorities, and alignment was present throughout the process

We will address in more detail the possible organizational structures in a later chapter; however, as part of the program strategy, the understanding of the stakeholders, skills required, and culture of collaboration is critical to address. Domain architectures can help address the problem of too much Business Analytics centralization, and they enable the program to address the issue of agility with a much finer discipline.

> "Agility is difficult to quantify. Some of these strategies are at the enterprise level, but some are locally owned and will develop over time. Recognize you can't completely centralize a large company and expect it to be agile. Centralization for the sake of cost reduction may ultimately result in a lack of agility that impacts efficiency and effectiveness in a negative way. If you centralize, make sure there are roadmaps to scale and support the broader enterprise as needs grow."
>
> — *Bill Frank, Manager, ITGF BI Practice, Johnson & Johnson*

As the number of these projects increased—and common analytics elements became recognized—we found ourselves developing similar analytics and leveraging information across the enterprise. Our domain architectures create an internal organizational structure for examining common analytics methodologies of value while preserving the agility to deliver targeted results.

The domain process develops the "information demand" that flows from the senior level of the organization down to the IT organization. The executives identify what is needed to activate an element of the business strategy. They determine who needs to be involved (e.g., Marketing, Sales). They establish the projected return on investment (ROI) and eliminate those elements that are not aligned to the business strategy.

This then becomes a project, composed of sub-projects, support functions, facilitation structures, and so on. The flow of command and planning cascades down from the high-level strategies through strategic planning to tactical planning, extending to IT where technical capabilities are determined. As the project responsibility cascades down, different teams perform the technical analysis to determine:

- The identification of the metrics
- The components (e.g., master data, metadata, business rules, analytics)
- The data warehouse
- The identification of the usable tools
- The IT mechanisms and technology required to facilitate the project

Throughout the process, a domain architect is the lead sponsor who can lead the decisions that continually align the projects to the business plan. The domain architect codifies:

- What the business needs
- How the pipeline of information is created
- How the solution is to be delivered

But the projected value to the organization was established up front, enabling the project teams to build according to the needs and technical details required. As a strong end-state vision for the program, the domain structure can help increase adoption, self-service, and a more pervasive analytic culture throughout the organization. However, throughout the process, fragmentation can arise if an evangelist and strategy

KEY CONCEPT

manager is not working across teams to identify common processes and elements and ensure teams are working across a coordinated framework. We feel that many organizations often overlook the role a Chief Analytics Officer, evangelist, or strategy manager will play in the ultimate success of the program. Having a key champion in a role to manage the coordination of strategy across teams, help prioritize projects, and identify areas of change is where the development of a common metrics framework can be realized. This role is often lacking in many organizations, but we feel it is a role that will be on the rise as the critical team member that will increase analytic success.

> "When you centralize too much, people lose accountability and responsibility. You can lose sight of what you are delivering and how agile that delivery might be. If there are competing projects, how do you resolve which one is of highest priority? If you are too segregated, everyone wants a separate solution. How do you provide value without duplicating solutions? If you are too centralized, you become too rigid. There's a balance that needs to be maintained between centralization and segmentation to preserve agility."
>
> —*Kay Van De Vanter, Information Management Domain Architect & Enterprise BI Architect, The Boeing Company*

Getting Started: Assessment of Strategy

Given that many organizations may have various fragmented strategies in the early stages, the most appropriate start to the development of a long-term Business Analytics Program Strategy is to understand the current state of the organization. A wide-reaching assessment of the various strategies, stakeholders, and expectations will provide the groundwork for understanding needs, requirements, and processes that will direct the program off to a successful start. This process includes:

- **Business Analytics vision and understanding assessment:** What is the current maturity level of the different parts of the organization, and what is their level of understanding about analytics?
- **Stakeholder identification and assessment:** Who are the stakeholders that will champion the program or who have the requirements that will drive the analytic needs?
- **Current state assessment:** Which business areas are more advanced in analytic capability and skill?
- **Technology assessment:** What technologies are already in place and supported throughout the business in terms of analytic tools and information silos?

Business Analytic Vision and Understanding

What is the current vision and understanding of analytics in your organization today? Is there a vision? Understanding the level of knowledge that exists in the organization around analytic capability and realization of how analytics can achieve increased performance—and the appetite for this knowledge—might be an eye-opening experience. In many cases, we have experienced that management may wish for what they believe is a simple dashboard to track specific focus areas of the company but not understand that the dashboard is just the tip of the iceberg and not comprehend the complexity of the multitude of technologies and data integrated from silos below the water. Business professionals may not realize that they could have the ability to predict future outcomes with today's innovative technologies. Understanding the levels of knowledge, vision, and appetite from various areas of the organization will help to establish a solid ground for creating a program strategy. Interviewing individuals that will become key stakeholders in the program is a first step to realizing analytic maturity.

Stakeholder Identification and Assessment

We think it's essential to employ a stakeholder analysis to identify individuals, subsidiaries, institutions, and other stakeholders involved in a project. This is something that needs to occur on a regular basis, however, because both people and priorities change over time. In early-stage programs, identifying top-priority initiatives and stakeholders will help you kick off the early wins needed to demonstrate the proof of what analytic vision can achieve. In programs that have experienced initial wins, identifying stakeholders that will help build out the roadmap in priority areas is an ongoing process that should be reviewed on a regular basis.

In the stakeholder analysis, you should target the business leaders who hold the business strategy at heart, but also seek to identify various target groups that will support the strategies and implementing mechanisms and speculate on their expected support or opposition to the program. Identifying who your champions are, as well as who your roadblocks might be, is a critical step to understanding what it will take to bring them together. This analysis is used at the preliminary stages of the various projects in order to incorporate interests and expectations of persons and groups significant to the project or program. Indeed, performing a stakeholder analysis is also key to establishing the communication mechanisms that are required over the long term.

Practically speaking, some of the exercises that can be done include:

1. Record the names of parties (e.g., groups, institutions, individuals, organizations, authorities) that are concerned in any way with the project. This includes individuals in influential positions and areas that may be affected by the problems addressed in the project.
2. Group the parties involved (individuals, organizations, and so on) and detail their motivations to facilitate discussion and analysis.

3. Select the groups with the strongest influence, and analyze the groups according to characteristics, problems affecting the group, needs, wishes, motives, and attitudes.
4. Map against key business strategies to decide whose interests and views are to be given priority in addressing the problems:
    ◦   Which are the groups most in need of assistance?
    ◦   Which interest groups should be supported to ensure positive development? In which way should they be considered?
    ◦   What conflicts would occur by supporting given interest groups, and what measures can be taken to avoid such conflicts?
5. Identify skilled professionals who will help support the analytic capability and data requirements.
6. Identify governance teams that exist in the organization and hold a stake in data governance processes.
7. Identify Information Management teams that support the data capture, storage, and technologies.
8. Interview the groups and stakeholders.

Many organizations often find that there are several teams and individuals supporting their various strategies. At this stage, realization that you cannot boil the ocean needs to be clear, but having a clear picture of the current stakeholder teams is necessary to define the vision. More detail on this process can be found in the "Practical Tips" section of this chapter.

> "Many, many smart people on both sides—on the innovation side—say 'we can do it better.' We are asking, '*How* do we make it better?' Sometimes they want to push it beyond what the organization was ready for."
>
> —*John Boyer*

Current State Assessment

As the stakeholder assessment is taking place, getting a vision on the current state across the stakeholder groups is going to provide a clearer path to the roadmap that is required. A first step is to look at the overall organization's maturity as it pertains to analytics. How quickly are decisions made? What strategies are in place? What type of analytic culture exists? What tools are used? You can use a model like the AQ Maturity Model to better understand the overall ability to use analytics to achieve successful outcomes.

A next step is to do a deeper dive—typically by business area or department. You will likely find that different departments may fall into different levels of the maturity model. This exercise should focus on a few key questions that should be answered:

- What are the top priorities and requirements for the business area and how are they connected to business strategy?
- Does the organization understand the paradigm of analytics?
- Does the area of the business already feel as though they well address their needs? How knowledgeable are they on analytics? What do they believe Business Analytics is?
- Does the area of the business already have the skills in place to meet analytic requirements?
- What processes are in place to collect information? What processes currently exist to gather analytic knowledge?
- Are there analytics already in place? Which sweet spots have already been addressed?
- What technologies are in place to support the initiative? What data sources are available, and who manages them? What do the source systems look like, and can meaningful analytics be gleaned from them?

Interviews with key stakeholders in the different areas can provide the insight to the organization on how to move forward in a strategic fashion.

Technology Assessment

Once you have a view of the various technologies that are used by the stakeholders and have completed interviews to understand the business processes in more detail, you can create a detailed map of the technologies that are required to ensure that the needs of the various teams are met. This map can help you determine where you have overlapping capabilities, where you have gaps, and how you can achieve a better total cost of ownership with the technologies in your organization. If you find various overlapping capabilities, ask the teams why they have chosen the technologies they need. If you find gaps, understand whether the cause is a lack of knowledge of the capabilities that are possible or that the solutions in place do not meet current needs. This process can help you understand whether the teams need to understand the "art of the possible" or if a view into the larger vision of the organization's strategy is required.

Creating the Kickoff Point

Most often, an event will trigger an analytic movement in an organization. Sometimes it may be the entry of a new executive who has prior experience with analytics. A market or business development may drive an immediate need. If an existing event trigger did not exist, a kickoff point can easily be created. In many cases, key stakeholders may not understand the art of the possible. An event that demonstrates the need and value may be an easy way to trigger an analytic movement. With the information now in hand from the assessment phase, the connection with a key stakeholder in need at the executive level can provide the shift required to begin a more formalized approach. You can create your own event to demonstrate proof of concept in a business context, with value assigned, to create heightened awareness and improve alignment across groups of stakeholders on a winning initiative.

- Create your own event. Create a moment in time.
- Bring stakeholders together to realize a common vision.
- Bring a third party in if that helps.
- Showcase a technology in context to demonstrate how it solves a business problem.
- Understand the vision among the teams.
- Use examples that help the stakeholders visualize or create the vision. Demonstrate an inventory of analytic solutions that can raise awareness and knowledge.
- Create a community of practice that drives the message around analytics— invite all who you think are change agents that can take the message back to stakeholders and/or would benefit from an understanding of what business analytics is.

> "One means to provide awareness and communicate BI capabilities and strategies is through a regularly scheduled meeting with representation from across the business domains and the BI and Data Management support areas. At our company, an 'Information Management Committee' meets periodically to discuss progress on major initiatives, demonstrate the latest new capabilities, and plan for upcoming research and development. Through an open, collaborative, and interesting forum, we reach out to our users to stay aligned with their needs and help ensure that we all have a shared vision.
>
> "By creating a vision for the art of the possible and collectively designing the vision, you will improve the success by moving in a common direction that is collectively understood and agreed upon."
>
> *—Brian Green*

Prioritization and Roadmap

After the initial envisioning event has been realized, the creation of a prioritized roadmap will help teams understand the path of "how to get there." Using the initial assessment, you can augment the identified sweet spots with the key identified champions and stakeholders in the business. Consider internal and external needs as well as information in the current systems of record and whether information outside these sources needs to be captured. Trigger a follow-up event with more detailed information to draw the roadmap with the prioritized parties. This can be as simple as rating the highest-value areas against ease of development to demonstrate how a roadmap of quick wins can be possible. Gain alignment on that vision with the team to ensure the approach is embraced. In the later part of this chapter, a special section that provides practical tips on how to create the roadmap can help you as a best practice example. Most important, the team needs to understand that this roadmap will change as the program evolves and as priorities change. It is an exercise that should be done frequently and one that is not cast in stone. Finally, the value in the roadmap is communicating the roadmap to the key stakeholders so that they understand the vision.

Metrics Framework and Measurement

Mapping goals to data is the hard part. And bringing teams together with a common measurement framework is even more difficult. The unique talent that is required to do this is exceptionally hard to find, which is why bringing together the right business acumen with analytic skill is critical to success. While most organizations realize they would like analytics that can help them make critical decisions, understanding the data measures and gaining consistency with other areas of measurements is difficult. Often, the business asks its technical teams to devise a dashboard and make changes iteratively. This can create a never-ending cycle of change. Often, you will also encounter other teams who analyze data but have slightly different measures and results. This is because a common metrics framework or agreement on how measures are created is not aligned. Creating a common metrics framework is political and difficult. Here are some best practices you will want to consider:

✓ **Executive-level involvement:** While every decision will likely not be made at the executive level, involvement at the executive level will often need to exist because it is often when information is rolled up at the executive level that inconsistencies occur.

✓ **Responsible party:** This exercise will not happen if someone is not tasked with the role. In some organizations, a person has been identified as being responsible for ironing out difficult decisions among stakeholders and teams. For example, what does "close date" mean for a sale? Is it the day the paperwork is signed? Is it the day the item is paid? The date it is shipped? The date it arrives? Creating a common metrics framework will involve discussion with various parties in an organization and is a process that will require strong negotiation skills and analytics talent.

> "This process of implementing a Business Analytics Strategy is sort of like creating a bonsai. The process of shaping and training the bonsai is actually an elusive thing that is impossible to fully document. There is no step-by-step cookbook of future tasks. Instead, it is a changing, growing, living thing that you guide. In a sense, you're bringing order to nature by helping the plant adapt to your vision."
>
> *—John Boyer*

✓ **Goals to data:** Understanding the requirements up front will help to determine which data is required. All too often, a lack of understanding of where data resides and what sources to tap into to get the answers is not realized until the project is under way. Analytic reports are created, answers are not found, and users gain little value.

✓ **Agility:** The standard waterfall process is most often not going to work with analytics. Agility, open communication, and iteration are required to be successful. We will talk more about this aspect in the process area of the book. Iterative rapid development with teams working together to achieve results will create higher success.

✓ **Don't allow the perfect to be the enemy of the good:** Recognize that building analytics is a highly iterative process that will often uncover flaws and issues with data, operational processes, business assumptions, and requirements.

Managing a Changing Strategy

Creating the initial roadmap is good, but recognize that it will change frequently with the needs of the business—and as your organization innovates and matures in the analytics journey. You will need to review the roadmap regularly and keep the program relevant. When this factor is not recognized early, you can lose agility—failing to change with the business priorities and not being forward-looking on technology innovations that can help in new areas will cause you to lose ground.

Creating an initial roadmap is a great start, but one of the most critical acknowledgments that a strategy needs to make is that the strategy will change dramatically—and possibly rapidly—over time. As business strategies change, new insights need to be gathered, and new ways of doing things need to be created. Automating current information processes will drive new efficiencies, but new processes continually need to be developed to capture any new information required to support and inform the business strategy.

Business Analytics tools are on the desktops of the users who are at the front lines of strategy change. These users expect immediate insight and the ability to use these tools as their needs change. However, if complex data challenges, lack of tool flexibility, lack of communication, or process challenges exist, the risk of the needs not being met in time can result in low confidence or an audience that disengages from the partnership.

Remember that another factor that influences how organizations deal with changing strategy within a Business Analytics Program is the maturity level of the analytics deployment. Depending on where an organization is with technology capability, analytic culture and organizational design will also affect the outcome of how quickly an organization can either proactively pursue a new strategy or react to changes in business needs.

The complexity of business alignment and technology change will grow as the program matures—the more you bring different areas of the business on board, the more you will need to manage the various team interests, opinions, and requirements. Creating a program that will be able to recognize when change is required and react and manage change over time is the goal. Having the individuals and teams tasked up front with keeping the strategy current and reviewing processes is necessary. Ensure this is understood up front in the visioning process—to realize value, a focus on this area is a requirement. Remaining agile will become a focus throughout the program—agile in terms of people, process, and technology. Remaining agile in onboarding new team members and groups, training new employees to become empowered with analytics, and changing processes that may have been right at their inception but have outlived their usefulness are highly important—as is agility in technology change and incorporation of new technologies into the platform. Constant reevaluation is necessary in all these areas—and we'll discuss each of these in the next few chapters of this book.

In the final part of this chapter, we look at a case study of how strategy successfully drives an organization that is mature in its analytics journey. We then explore some practical tips on how to create your roadmap and review a checklist of key components of strategy in your Business Analytics Program that will help to put you on a path to success. This discussion will then lead into our next Key to Success: how to demonstrate and measure value continually throughout the maturity of your Business Analytics Program.

Case Study on Strategy: Mueller, Inc.

From guest author Mark Lack, Manager,
Strategy Analytics & Business Intelligence, Mueller, Inc.

*Mueller, Inc. uses a balanced scorecard approach
in its Business Analytics system to monitor
customer satisfaction and improve operational processes*

> "The key to sustainability is the ability to execute strategy. Our Business Analytics system provides the communication platform to set our balanced scorecard strategy, communicate goals, measure results, and reflect back with the velocity required in today's economy."
>
> —*Phillip Arp, Chief Financial Officer, Mueller, Inc.*

Mueller Overview

Founded over 75 years ago in Ballinger, Texas, Mueller, Inc. is a privately held company employing more than 600 people. It began as a family-owned sheet metal company selling water cisterns to local farmers and ranchers, but over the years the business expanded into other sheet metal products related to the building industry. Today Mueller, Inc. is a customer-focused manufacturer and distributor of pre-engineered metal building and residential metal roofing products in the southwestern and central United States with three manufacturing facilities and 34 locations in Texas, Louisiana, New Mexico, and Oklahoma. Its success hinges upon maintaining a strong financial base while continuing its long-term growth rate through satisfied customers.

Maintaining that strong financial basis in a company tied to the construction industry takes unusual skill and business acumen in today's economy. In 2000, the company decided to streamline the retail sales, manufacturing, and distribution processes as part of its overall strategy to manage growth and support the continued evolution of its end-user strategy. This strategic decision transformed both how the organization created product and how it responded to its growing community of customers. Mueller, Inc. has transformed its sheet metal products company into a customer-focused manufacturing and distribution organization by utilizing Business Analytics as its strategic information tool. With a strong focus on strategy and how to operationally execute on that strategy using analytics with a balanced scorecard approach, Mueller has been able to benefit from real results:

- 113 percent return on investment within 12 months
- $782,000 annual net benefit from the investment in analytics

How did they do it?

The Balanced Scorecard Approach

> "One of the critical contributors to our success has been the ability to provide every employee at Mueller with the relevant information they need to make optimized decisions every day."
>
> —*Bryan Davenport, President, Mueller, Inc.*

Mueller's strategic decision focus on the end-user sales channel triggered the creation of a strategy to align information to business goals with the development of a cultural and organizational behavior that would drive the strategic use of technology to execute the strategy. This supported a technology change that included a migration to a new enterprise resource planning (ERP) environment to reflect the business changes in processes and operations. The ERP system enabled the company to collect a wealth of detailed, operational data that Mueller had not previously tracked. This data provided an opportunity to analyze the business, monitor performance, and optimize management decisions for reinforcing its customer-centric culture.

To achieve this, the Mueller team introduced a strategy manager who works closely with the CEO on priorities and deployed a Business Analytics solution to identify and monitor a range of key performance metrics to support a balanced scorecard strategy. The balanced scorecard analytics approach defines a set of key strategic metrics to provide management with insights into how the organization is performing. By aligning metrics to key outcomes and then monitoring these metrics, management gains a better understanding of how the complex supply chain and distribution network are functioning, as well as an increased ability to measure customer satisfaction. Where performance is lower than expected, Mueller focuses its efforts on improving operational efficiencies and business results.

This Business Analytics Strategy improves the quality of information that management receives, reducing the complexity of decision making and offering a better communication strategy of goals throughout the organization.

To deliver the balanced scorecard metrics, Muller had several important business objectives that would streamline its decision-making processes. It needed to:

- **Drive a business alignment strategy through the development of balanced scorecard metrics:** The company chose to implement a balanced scorecard framework to link its Business Analytics Strategy to operational execution and to empower every employee to make decisions to improve the quality and delivery of products.
- **Drive a culture of performance with key metrics that delivered customer feedback processes:** To reduce costs and increase customer satisfaction, Mueller began formally monitoring its customer satisfaction levels by tying customer survey reports to its key Business Analytics metrics.

- **Enhance information and analytic systems:** Mueller needed to extend its ERP investment to expand insight across all operations through a consolidated platform for strategy, analytics, Business Intelligence, and planning.

Developing Best Practices at Mueller

> "To fulfill our business purpose, we needed a clear strategy backed by a culture that would use a variety of capabilities that would help us very quickly deliver value and transform our data assets to information for enterprise decision making."
>
> —*Mark Lack, Manager, Strategy Analytics & Business Intelligence, Mueller, Inc.*

Transforming its business strategy through the implementation of Business Analytics required an ongoing commitment to refine internal behavior that would drive the processes of streamlining data collection as the company developed new reports for its management and operational personnel. This transformation permitted the organization to establish some best practices that continue to deliver benefits to the company. A few of these best practices include:

- ✓ **Management sponsorship:** Gaining the right executive management buy-in at an early stage and establishing a vision for Business Analytics drove its adoption across the company.
- ✓ **Alignment with the various stakeholders:** Establishing the right relationships to gain early alignment to business goals and develop the right working relationships to effectively create and monitor business goals ensured needs were captured and can easily evolve.
- ✓ **Prioritizing initiatives and strategically rolling them out:** Strategically working with the stakeholders, prioritizing the highest-value initiatives, and ensuring those initiatives are rolled out to get the visibility needed by the various business owners in a clear way created a process that allowed Mueller to achieve the vision. A big bang strategy would not have worked—instead, a roadmap of successes created with the right group of stakeholders allowed the organization to achieve the vision.

Proven Business Benefits

A Nucleus Research ROI study[3] revealed that enhanced customer and supply chain focus at Mueller has resulted in tangible ROI results of 113 percent within 12 months, with an annual net benefit of $782,000 from the investment in Business Analytics (Figure 4). The benefits of the Business Analytics approach at Mueller included:

---

[3] *ROI Case Study: IBM Smarter Commerce, Mueller, Inc. (Report L115).* Nucleus Research. Boston, MA: October 2011.

Return on Investment Summary

Annual ROI: 113%

Payback period:
1 year

Average annual benefit:
$782,000

Total Three-Year Benefits

Direct	$2,250,000
Indirect	$96,000
Total	$2,346,000

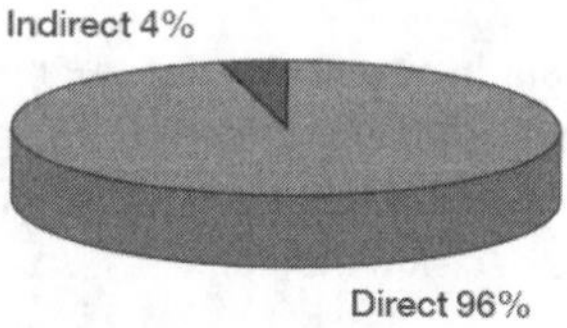

Indirect 4%

Direct 96%

Source: *Nucleus Research ROI Case LX - IBM Business Analytics, Mueller, Inc.*

Figure 4: Results Achieved with Mueller, Inc.'s Business Analytics System

- **Strengthened customer satisfaction:** By monitoring and analyzing customer surveys, Mueller increased its customer satisfaction rates and sped product delivery using customer satisfaction data and feeding back improvement suggestions to operational teams.
- **Streamlined information delivery:** Mueller's Business Analytics approach accelerated information delivery from weeks to days, enabling employees to analyze data when relevant for better decision making.
- **Business process tracking:** Mueller's information system now performs a more rapid identification and tracking of business processes, increasing the return on assets by 20 percent.

Building a successful business strategy requires foresight, vision, and commitment to monitor and adjust all the key metrics of the business. By providing focus on business strategies and providing relevant information to employees across the organization to monitor their performance and identify areas where improvements can be made, Mueller has been able to maintain lean staffing levels and drive improvements in product manufacturing and delivery. They credit the close linkage to the business strategy and stakeholders as a key success factor to ensure the right information is being communicated from the start, increasing adoption and buy-in to the program.

Strategy: Practical Tips for Identifying, Assessing, and Prioritizing Metrics

Special insert authored by Roland Mosimann,
CEO of AlignAlytics and co-author of *The Performance Manager*

Defining standard metrics and turning them into something measurable and relevant is not a simple task. Many challenges and pitfalls have caused metrics initiatives to fail, including some the following:

- Having too many ("laundry list") or too few ("too general")
- Not providing the proper context to understand root cause and trade-offs between dependencies (e.g., cost reduction vs. revenue growth)
- Having too few relative and derived vs. absolute metrics (e.g., %, $/#, Index)
- Finding metrics with the same name but different meanings or different names with the same meaning
- Not assigning clear ownership for defining a metric or lack of accountability for managing a metric's performance
- Not showing clearly how metrics will "help me do my job" vs. "just another corporate program"
- Failing to properly source information, whether quantitative or qualitative

Addressing these challenges requires a strong partnership between the IT team and the business managers. Business managers define what business objectives they are seeking to achieve and what performance to measure, and the IT and analytics teams help to connect those metrics to the reality of the data.

Identifying Metrics That Matter

The framework described in the book *The Performance Manager*[4] is a helpful tool for identifying the metrics that matter most to the business. How? By understanding how bottom-up decisions "connect to" top-down strategic goals and objectives. Although the bottom-up is described first, you can start with either top or bottom and ideally do both iteratively.

Bottom-Up Metrics

The foundational concept of the book is an enterprise framework of decisions that drive outcomes. Each decision area is briefly described by function (Finance, Marketing, Sales, and so on) together with a corresponding information "sweet spot" of (a) goals, (b) metrics, and (c) a hierarchical set of dimensions. These templates of decisions and information can be used to guide the conversation with a combined team of IT and business managers. This is the bottom-up view.

---

[4] Roland Mosimann, Patrick Mosimann, and Meg Dussault. *The Performance Manager: Proven Strategies for Turning Information into Higher Business Performance*. Ottawa, Canada: Cognos, 2010.

Let's use an example from the book: the sales results decision area. In Table 4, the revenue management goals of the organization are listed with the corresponding metrics ($/%) by which these goals will be measured and the underlying metrics and dimensions by which they will be created.

Goals	Metrics	Dimensions	
New Customer Sales ($)	Avg. Sales per Order ($)	Billing Customer	Product SKU
Sales Growth (%)	Avg. Units per Order (#)	Industry Group	Product Line
Sales Orders ($)	Credit Balance ($)	Industry	Brand
	Credit Limit ($)	Category	SKU
	Customers (#)	Customer Name	
	Lost Customer Count (#)		Sales Channel Partners
	New Customer Count (#)	Customer Location	Sales Channel Type
	New Product Sales ($)	Region	Sales Partner
	Sales Order Count (#)	State/Province	
	Units Ordered (#)	County	Sales Organization
		Postal/Zip Code	Sales Region
			Sales Territory
		Fiscal Week	Sales Code
		Fiscal Year	
		Quarter	Ship-To Location
		Month	Region
		Week	Sate/Province
			County
		Marketing Segment	City
		Market Segment	Postal/Zip Code
		Micro-Segment	

Table 4: Sales Results Decision Area

Sales results information across the five basic components of the business—product, customer, territory, channel, and time—provide operational detail in support of financial revenue trends and variances. Insights gained inform decisions around sales resource and incentive adjustments to meet targets and also to improve predictability of future performance.

Use these templates to spark discussion around what types of decisions are being made, what outcomes or goals your team is trying to impact, and how they measure success today. Also try to determine the information sources available, whether that information is being systemically managed (scrubbed, integrated, enhanced with business rules, and so on), and how it is being delivered to the decision maker. You can think of this exercise as an information supply chain with three core processes: Information Sourcing, Information Management, and Information Delivery—a concept that will come in handy later in assessing and prioritizing your metrics and analytics efforts (see sections below).

Top-Down Metrics

The key to a top-down framework of metrics is defining the core drivers of your strategic goals and objectives. This can be done in different ways, for example by using a strategy map or a strategic planning document and organizing its content into a causality hierarchy or structure. The Performance Manager also provides a top-down framework represented by four areas for managing performance:

- Financial Management: Are we performing to shareholder expectations?
- Revenue Management: Are we driving revenue growth effectively?
- Expense Management: Are we managing operational expenses effectively?
- Long-Term Asset Management: Are we managing long-term assets effectively to affect future revenue and expense management capabilities?

These performance areas also reflect the "several interrelated balancing acts: between leading [operational] and lagging [financial] indicators; between revenue and expense trade-offs; between short-term and long-term resource allocations; and between top-down and bottom-up management processes"[5]. Figure 5 illustrates the primary drivers of these performance areas.

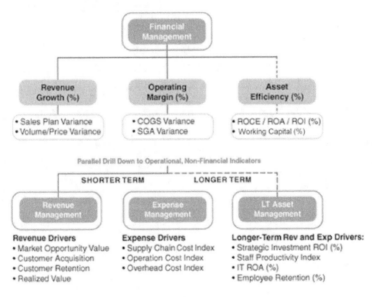

Figure 5: Top-Down Performance Framework

Let's use the Revenue Management performance area as an example and review the four underlying performance drivers:

- Market Opportunity Value = Which markets are most attractive for revenue growth and margin?
- Customer Acquisition = Are we competing successfully and gaining new customers and/or growing our share of wallet?

---

5 Ibid.

- Customer Retention = Are we able to meet customers' expectations and retain their business most effectively?
- Customer Acquisition = Are we realizing the optimal value from our customer relationships?

Use these questions to discuss what drivers are most important and what metrics would help measure their performance. Even if you don't have consensus yet on exact metrics, recognizing the drivers and their characteristics keeps the process moving forward.

"Connecting the Dots" Between Top-Down and Bottom-Up

By linking the top-down and bottom-up perspectives together, as illustrated in Figure 6, you've "connected the dots" between strategic, financial, and operational metrics and

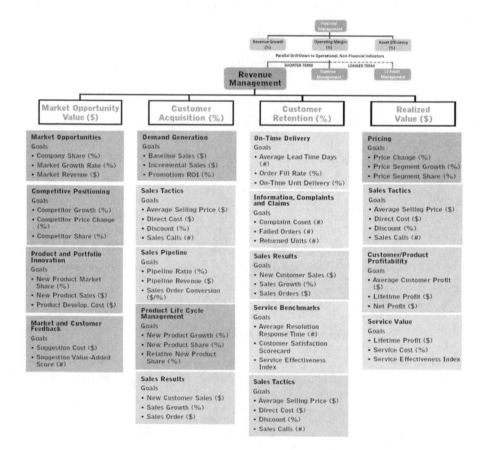

Figure 6: Revenue Management Performance Drivers and Decision Areas

Goals	Metrics	Dimensions

Company Share (%)
Market Growth Rate (%)
Market Revenue ($)
	Market Growth (%)
	Market Profit ($)
	Market Unit Volume (#)
	Profit (%)
	Sales ($)
	Unit Volume Sales (#)
		Fiscal Month
		  Year
		  Quarter
		  Month
		
		Industries
		  SIC 2-Digit
		  SIC 4-Digit
		
		Marketing Areas
		  Region
		  Area
		
		Marketing Segment
		  Market Segment
		  Micro-Segment
		
		Product Brand
		  Product Line
		  Brand
		
		Sales Organization
		  Sales Region
		  Sales Territory
		  Org. Code

Table 2: Market Opportunities Decision Area

created a set of "cascaded metrics." This addresses the challenge of having too many or too few metrics.

Revisiting the sales decision area, the discussion expands beyond the shorter-term view to include how broader revenue portfolio patterns are evaluated (Table 2). For example, are strategic assumptions still valid for achieving customer acquisition and penetration objectives that drive longer-term revenue goals?

Further insight into revenue performance is gained when sales results are compared with market opportunities. Are results consistent with market share goals, in the right market segments?

Likewise, for each decision area added with other metrics included, the linkage between longer-term goals and objectives and shorter-term decisions and outcomes can be made, thereby extending the "line of sight" between the two (Figure 7). Identifying the metrics that matter by using a cascaded logic helps improve forecasting accuracy and create early warning signals for shorter-term plans and targets while also providing longer-term signals for strategic course correction.

Enabling Collaboration with Metrics and Context

Identifying the metrics that matter also means understanding the network of decision makers that share common drivers and outcomes. The right metrics should enable collaborative decision-making cycles that result from sharing common performance

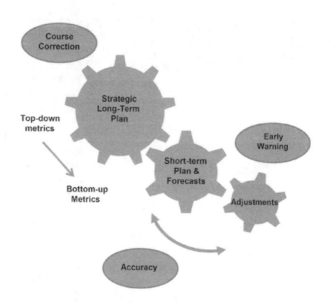

Figure 7: Linking Metrics to Extend "Line of Sight" from Short to Long Term

goals: setting goals and targets, measuring results and monitoring outcomes, analyzing root causes, and "course correcting" future goals and targets.

It also helps to identify different collaboration needs based on different decision roles with different work responsibilities. A decision role can be derived from a person's work function (e.g., Marketing, Sales, Purchasing) and his or her job type (e.g., executive, manager, professional, analyst). Work responsibilities can be divided into three basic levels of involvement: Primary, Contributory, and Status. The Performance Manager templates identify which managers are likely to use the decision area and show relevant decision roles and work responsibilities, as Table 3 illustrates for the sales results decision area.

Understanding the varied roles and responsibilities that need to collaborate to optimize overall performance also helps avoid a "one-size-fits-all" solution to the information process itself. Instead, it suggests the need for more than one type of capability, and a significant value to the organization is the identification of which capability is best suited for which role. Executives may rely on performance scorecards and dashboards; business analysts may rely on detailed BI reports; financial analysts may rely on forecasting spreadsheets derived with complex algorithms and "what if" capability. The tools and information slices must match the needs that the job requires.

The different roles, workflow, collaboration, and respective capabilities and information slices provide holistic answers to the three core questions every decision-making cycle needs:

Function	Decision roles	Primary work	Contributory	Status
Marketing				
	Executives			*
	Managers		*	
	Analysts		*	
	Professionals		*	
Sales				
	Executives	*		
	Managers	*		
	Analysts	*		
	Professionals	*		
Audit				
	Executives			*
	Managers	*		
	Professionals	*		
Finance				
	Executives			*
	Analysts		*	
Customer Service				
	Executives		*	
	Analysts		*	
Operations/Production				
	Executives			*
Product Development				
	Executives			*
	Analysts		*	
Customer Service				
	Executives	*		
	Analysts	*		

Table 3: Sales Results Decision Roles Map

- "How are we doing?" typically relies on scorecards and dashboards or real-time monitoring that can provide information about the present at your fingertips.
- "Why?" relies on historical data presented through reporting and analysis.
- "What should we be doing?" relies on planning and forecasting, what-if scenarios, and predictive skills and techniques that roll up and extend the information paradigms of other departments and give a view and plan into the future.

It's the process of integrating these capabilities that creates agility. This step process permits the organization to respond to the changes in the business. And this process of integration will require consistency across the full network of performance managers, whether within a single department or across several. This consistency includes having the proper context for defining and analyzing the "metrics that matter," not just from a functional bottom-up view but also from the cross-functional perspective that shares a common performance area such as revenue management or a performance driver like customer acquisition. Context or dimensions is what frames the metric and the root cause analysis. For example, if sales results are down, for which products and customers, in what territories, in which channel, and over what time frame?

In some ways "context is everything," and for effective collaboration common dimensions must mean the same thing across each decision role and function involved. Recognizing this fact should guide your definitions of metrics and help prioritize any information management efforts such as master data management (MDM) and data governance. As an example, the most effective collaboration across the four performance drivers of revenue management would require a common context across at least four functions: Marketing, Sales, Development, and Customer Service, as we saw in Figure 5.

Assessing and Prioritizing Metrics

A helpful technique for determining which metrics to develop first is to assess the business's demand for metrics in terms of its relative value and compare this with an assessment of IT's supply of underlying information quality in terms of how well it meets this need. The resulting demand and supply analysis acts as a cost–benefit proxy for prioritizing metrics initiatives.

Assessing Demand Using Value and Gap

The demand side captures how business perceives the relative value and importance of the decisions they need to make, including the metrics used in that decision area. Creating an assessment is relatively straightforward. In the example in Figure 8, the relative value of each decision area is a function of (a) the level of Analytics Quotient (AQ) maturity (based on a best practice example) and (b) the importance of making further improvements, both using a four-point rating scale. Thus, a low AQ maturity coupled with a very high improvement rating would represent the highest potential value[6] coded numerically from lowest (1) to highest (4).

Assessment of Value & Gap by Performance Driver & Decision Area										
Performance Driver	Decision Area	Decision Area KPIs	Value Index	Value - Maturity	Value - Import- ance	Average Gap	Gap - Availa- bility	Gap - Relia- bility	Gap - Value- Add	Gap - Adop- tion
Revenue Growth (%)	01.01. Income Statement	1) Actual vs Plan Variance ($/%) 2) Net Sales ($) 3) Operating Profit/EBIT ($/%)	3	4	4	2	1	1	4	3
Revenue Growth (%)	01.02. Drill Down Variance	1) Profit Change ($/%) 2) Sales Change ($/%) 3) Volume/Price/Mix Variance ($/%)	4	1	4	3	4	3	2	2
Revenue Growth (%)	03.05 Sales Plan Variance	1) Sales Order ($) 2) Sales Plan ($/%)	4	2	4	2	2	2	2	3
Customer Acquisition (%)	02.03. Product Life Cycle Mgt	1) New Product Growth % 2) New Product Share % 3) Relative New Product Share (%)	3	2	2	3	3	2	3	3
Customer Acquisition (%)	02.05. Demand Generation	1) Baseline Sales $ 2) Incremental Sales $ 3) Promotions ROI %	3	2	3	3	2	2	3	3
Customer Acquisition (%)	03.01. Sales Results	1) New Customer Sales ($) 2) Sales Growth (%) 3) Sales Order ($)	2	3	2	3	2	3	3	3
Customer Acquisition (%)	03.03. Sales Tactics	1) Average Selling Price $ 2) Direct Cost $ 3) Discount (%) 4) Sales Calls #	3	2	3	2	2	2	1	1
Customer Acquisition (%)	03.04. Sales Pipeline	1) Pipeline Ratio (%) 2) Pipeline Revenue $ 3) Sales Order Conversion %	3	3	3	3	3	3	3	3

Figure 8: Demand Value and Gap Assessment Matrix

---

[6] An inverse gap integer is used to normalize low maturity + high importantce = highest rating.

At the same time, an analytic capability assessment provides a better understanding of the relative effort or cost of further improvement. In our example, we evaluate four factors:

- **Availability:** Is all the needed information available?
- **Reliability:** How reliable is the information?
- **Value Add:** How much additional value beyond the initial source data does the information provide?
- **Adoption:** How well are analytics used in decision making?
- Gaps in each of these factors would suggest different solution types and costs. For example, missing data sources might require significant investments into new processes and/or transaction systems, whereas a need for greater reliability might require additional information management efforts. On the other hand, if neither of these factors has gaps but there are value-add or adoption challenges, those might be solved with relatively smaller investments into new tools (e.g., predictive, visualization, what if) or training and change management efforts.

Assessing Supply Using the Information Supply Chain

The next step is to evaluate the supply side by understanding the underlying "data landscape" in terms of the different IT assets and grouping these into an Information Supply Chain (ISC) made up of:

- Information Sources = Where does the data come from?
- Information Management = What is done to it?
- Information Delivery = How does it get to users?

Figure 9 illustrates this concept.

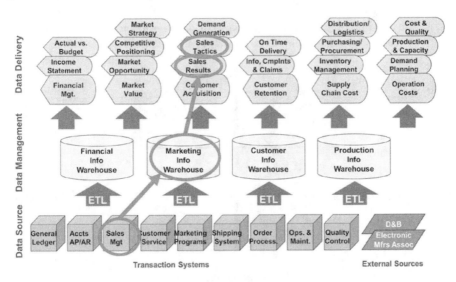

Figure 9: IT Assets with ICS Roll-Up

Defining ISCs that we can map to specific decision areas makes it easier to understand what a solution for improvement might require, especially for a business audience that can relate to the concept of supply chain effectiveness. IT can now rate the quality of those assets from a technical perspective, including factors that impact total cost of ownership, as Figure 10 illustrates.

Prioritizing Metric Deployment Using a Heat Map

Bringing the demand and supply assessments together creates a framework for defining a deployment road map (Figure 11). Starting with the demand side, a comparison of relative value vs. relative gap identifies quick win (high value, small gap) and strategic (high value, large gap) initiatives. The other two quadrants represent more tactical (lower value, small gap) deployments or potentially even ones to be dropped or changed (lower value, large gap).

Assessment of Information Supply Chains					
ISC	ISC Rating	Reliability	Availability	Compatibility	Scalability
ISC Actuals & Forecast (Fin)	3	2	3	3	3
ISC Cust. & Prod. Profitability	2	1	1	2	2
ISC Income Statement	1	1	1	1	1
ISC Product Development	3	1	1	4	4
ISC Sales Pipeline	2	2	2	2	2
ISC Sales Plan	1	1	1	1	2
ISC Sales Plan Variance	1	1	1	1	2
ISC Sales Tactics	3	3	1	4	4

Figure 10: ISC Assessment

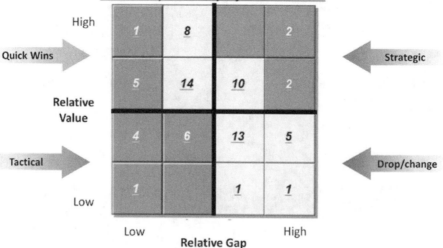

Figure 11: Value/Gap Heat Map by Decision Area

For the high value metrics, further consideration based on the ISC ratings helps set priorities that can be turned into a road map over time, as Figures 12 and 13 illustrate.

With this approach, you can pragmatically compare the "apples-to-apples" metrics for understanding the data generated by the silos within the organization. It achieves these metrics through consistent definitions that reflect the organization's overall informational sweet spots—not just the sweet spots identified within any particular silo. It achieves a metric framework by which the Business Analytics Program Team can then tie the day-to-day execution processes within the organization to the business strategy its executives are demanding.

This process is achievable and repeatable, so that as the business strategy changes over time, the organization has built-in agility to respond and adapt to the change.

Priority by Decision Area											
Performance Driver	Decision Area	Value Index	Value Maturity	Value Importance	Average Gap	Gap - Availability	Gap - Reliability	Gap - Value Add	Gap - Adoption	PRIORITY	ISC Rating
Revenue Growth (%)	03.05 Sales Plan Variance	4	2	4	2	2	2	2	3	1	1
Revenue Growth (%)	01.01. Income Statement	3	4	4	2	1	1	4	3	1	1
Customer Acquisition (%)	03.01. Sales Results	2	3	2	3	2	3	3	3	1	1
Revenue Growth (%)	01.02. Drill Down Variance	4	1	4	3	4	3	2	2	2	3
Customer Acquisition (%)	02.05. Demand Generation	3	2	3	3	2	2	3	3	3	2
Customer Acquisition (%)	03.04. Sales Pipeline	3	2	3	3	3	3	3	3	3	2
Customer Acquisition (%)	02.03. Product Life Cycle Mgt	3	2	2	3	3	2	3	3	4	3
Customer Acquisition (%)	03.03. Sales Tactics	3	2	3	2	2	2	1	1	4	3

Figure 12: Demand Assessment Heat Map

Program for Business Analytics														
ACTIVITIES			TIME PERIODS											
			P1	P2	P3	P4	P5	P6	P7	P8	P9	P10	P11	P12
Skills														
	Staffing & Training														
Infrastructure														
	Data Analysis & Data Modeling														
	Data Mart Design & Construction														
Business Analytics Initiatives														
Performance Driver	Decision Area	PRIORITY	Implementation Plan											
Revenue Growth (%)	03.05 Sales Plan Variance	1												
Revenue Growth (%)	01.01. Income Statement	1												
Customer Acquisition (%)	03.01. Sales Results	1												
Revenue Growth (%)	01.02. Drill Down Variance	2												
Customer Acquisition (%)	02.05. Demand Generation	3												
Customer Acquisition (%)	03.04. Sales Pipeline	3												
Customer Acquisition (%)	02.03. Product Life Cycle Mgt	4												
Customer Acquisition (%)	03.03. Sales Tactics	4												

Figure 13: Metrics Deployment Plan

Strategy Checklist

The strategy chapter discussed a number of program areas that should be considered in the creation of your strategy. Use this checklist to see which areas might be useful to consider as you plan your strategy in your organization:

- ✓ How connected to the priorities of the business is the program today? Do you have a way to identify and manage changing priorities?
- ✓ Are key stakeholders from business, IT, and finance connected and collaborating?
- ✓ Is there a vision and understanding of how analytics can improve outcomes in your organization?
- ✓ Have you assessed which business areas are advanced in analytic capability and skill? Have you assessed which areas require improvement?
- ✓ What technologies are in place today that can be leveraged, extended, or integrated?
- ✓ How do you prioritize initiatives today?
- ✓ Is there a roadmap with identified sweet spots of information that reflects the priorities and key objectives of the organization?
- ✓ Are you able to manage changing strategies and reflect business priorities as they change?

Chapter 2
Key #2: Value

In the first chapter, we spoke about how strategy will be the driving force to making a Business Analytics Program work. Understanding key business strategies will help to prioritize the work that must be done to achieve the highest levels of value. However, sometimes value is hard to determine and quite often is not measured in a Business Analytics Program—leaving the program at risk of derailment. This chapter will help you understand how to measure value and learn how the documentation and demonstration of value can be managed.

What is the value that a Business Analytics Program returns to our organizations? How do we define that value and demonstrate that it's been realized? How do we measure value over time, so our organizations can support the processes and funding that will sustain it? Why is measuring value so important for success?

> "We need to show value so we can grow the program; navigate politics and culture; build on the successes; keep future funding; to show value even for support and maintenance. Why? Because there are other projects that want a piece of the funding. If everyone understands the value, the program will mature more quickly because people will understand why they need to jump on board or change the way they do things. You will not run into funding issues. Yet value is often treated as an afterthought or a project that someone should work on when they have spare time in many Business Analytics Programs."
>
> —Bill Frank

For a Business Analytics Program to succeed, we've found it's necessary not only to address these questions but also to communicate the answers in the business language that our management understands and accepts. If you can show the marketing manager, sales manager, or other domain area managers how they will benefit from analytics, it is much easier to enlist their help and work together collaboratively. Frequently, that terminology includes the phrase *return on investment (ROI)*—the measurable level of value that is created, over time, after the implementation has been completed. A second common term is *total cost of ownership (TCO)*—the sum of all costs associated with the purchase, development, and implementation of a proposed process or solution.

> "Our organization regards BI and Analytics like oxygen. How do you put a value on oxygen?"
>
> —*Brian Green*

Sometimes, Business Analytics initiatives fail to achieve value. Is it because of flaws in the implementation? Are they just *oversold* to management and expectations are not in line with reality? Is it because the business strategy changes more quickly than the project? Or is it because of a lack of understanding of the value that these initiatives deliver?

If stakeholders or management don't understand the components—both tangible and intangible—of a project's value, funding can be difficult to come by. Likewise, if they don't understand how the Business Analytics Program delivers value, the projects managed by the program will also falter. Instead, politics, resistance to change, cultural norms, and other factors will rule, and inertia will hamper both.

How can you preempt these potential obstacles? The first step is to define the business value of the Business Analytics Program and its projects—with potential `incremental targets and benchmarks. It is important to continue capturing value as the program evolves and to communicate the value over time. In this way, teams will recognize the value of their investments by funding people and resources so that those investments will continue.

In this chapter, we talk about a few key areas that are critical success factors for the BI Program, including:

- The business value hierarchy
  - ◦ IT efficiency
  - ◦ Business efficiency
  - ◦ Business effectiveness
- Evolving focus on value and maturity
  - ◦ Defining a business case
  - ◦ Documenting a value portfolio
  - ◦ BI metrics and feedback

Describing Value: The Business Value Hierarchy

In our previous book on strategy, we discussed the challenge of conveying value to the enterprise. We know, for example, that management is focused on projecting the Total Cost of Ownership when considering the implementation of new tools or systems, so IT is constantly monitoring the cost of product licenses, consulting, hardware, and operating expenses.

At the same time, management is also looking for a reasonable Return on Investment. The problem is how to bring these concepts into a framework that actually describes the *value* of a Business Analytics Program to the organization over time. This challenge even more difficult for the Business Analytics Program when the organization is early in its analytics maturity and is made up of fragmented and siloed projects.

Consequently, providing time and resources to understand value is a key component of reaching success at a more rapid pace. The Business Analytics Program needs to establish mechanisms whereby value is defined and agreed to up front (potentially even before the program is created, as well as when each new project kicks off) and is recorded across teams in a collective fashion.

> "Someone once said, 'If you're not keeping score, you're only practicing.' To put it another way, if you don't have a goal, there's no sense in measuring your progress. So, if you do have something you value—say, for example, a Business Analytics Program—you can demonstrate your success by measuring your progress. If your score is less than perfect, you know that you need to make adjustments."
>
> —*John Boyer*

The book *The Performance Manager*[1] defines a construct, known as the **business value hierarchy**, for understanding value that can be applied to Business Analytics. The hierarchy, which is depicted in Figure 14, demonstrates the various levels of value that

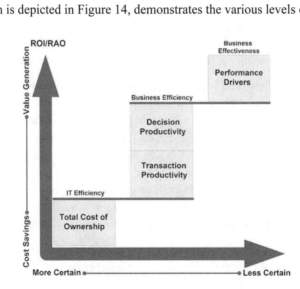

Figure 14: The Business Value Hierarchy[2]

[1] Roland Mosimann, Patrick Mosimann, and Meg Dussault. *The Performance Manager: Proven Strategies for Turning Information into Higher Business Performance*. Ottawa, Canada: Cognos, 2010.
[2] Ibid.

should be defined, measured, and monitored throughout the life of the Business Analytics Program. The business value hierarchy helps management to see the larger picture of our strategy and better understand the value of the different stages of the program's maturity. Measuring value helps executives see the direct link between actions taken and the strategy they have defined to determine whether the current tactics are effective.

This hierarchy explains that there are three levels of value that need to be measured. Some are easier to measure (such as IT efficiency), while others (such as business effectiveness) can be more difficult. At the same time, each provides a different business value—whether it is cost savings or value generation. These three levels of value need to be defined up front—from an overall program perspective as well as project by project—and measured and monitored as the program evolves:

- **IT efficiency:** Typically cost savings and time savings that can be garnered from better utilizing technology. An example of this measurement might be the Total Cost of Ownership of a technology deployment.
- **Business efficiency:** Measurement of increases in productivity, time savings, and the ability to do a job better. An example of this might be for analysts to be able to turn around standard reports more quickly, thereby providing them the time to do more strategic analysis in new areas.
- **Business effectiveness:** The business outcomes that are achieved by the implementation of the technology. An example might be a 20 percent increase in sales because the sales people now have visibility into their customer information that allowed them to determine new buying patterns. IT effectiveness can also increase at this point and be quantified—now that technology is realizing full potential and IT teams are working smarter.

Our experience shows that you can apply the Strategy Framework discussed in the Introduction to the business value hierarchy to get a clear picture of the areas that need to be in focus for a Business Analytics Program to capture all levels of value (Figure 15). IT efficiency can be achieved by having the right technology strategy in place to achieve the best TCO for the organization. This in turn creates business efficiencies when the automation of manual processes is achieved and realized, when users are trained in the tool capabilities, and when individuals are sharing best practices and information and focusing on new business process rather than working in silos of information. Finally, with alignment of the business strategy to the analytics initiative, business effectiveness can be achieved and measured.

Typical Maturity Patterns of Value Realization

Many organizations have typically been unstructured in their means to collect, measure, and communicate value, as value is often collected after the fact vs. planned from the

BI Excellence Framework

Figure 15: The BI Excellence Framework[3]

beginning of the initiative. However, by learning best practices from other organizations, through books such as this one, or by participating in frequent user groups, networking, or conferences, you can shorten your time to maturity. If we take the example of the Analytics Quotient Maturity Model, often organizations at an early level of analytics maturity would be forward-thinking to invest not only in the infrastructure but also in the organizational processes that will deliver, define, measure, and communicate recognizable business-related results. That investment takes time to achieve, through collaboration, metric analysis, key performance indicators (KPIs), and so on. Pick near-term as well as longer-term value measurements so that management can assess value over time.

In the early stages of maturity, organizations tend not to be well aligned across the enterprise in the way they might define value:

- Business units running their own analytics initiatives may be able to measure the business effectiveness in immediate payback for a project but may have difficulty demonstrating the long-term value. Further, their various silos of duplicate efforts actually increase the costs as Business Analytics becomes a series of disconnected projects as opposed to a program.
- IT organizations might be able to measure the cost and usage of a tool or set of tools used and quantify some of the efficiencies gained through automation of manual processes, but they often can have difficulty determining the various business results they will achieve due to the outcomes that are seen as a result of increased visibility and insight. Measurement might also be skewed due to poor

---

[3] John Boyer, Bill Frank, Brian Green, Tracy Harris, and Kay Van De Vanter. *Business Intelligence Strategy: A Practical Guide for Achieving BI Excellence."* Ketchum, ID: MC Press, 2010.

benchmarking practices from the beginning or siloed applications throughout the organization.

Resolution: A partnership and focused effort among business owners, analysts, and IT to consistently measure the various levels of value would help bridge this gap. This goal would require investment in a program owner who would coordinate the efforts between the teams.

Where does an organization start? The initial step is to put in place a process that will help build a business case for each initiative in the early stages, so you can have a target related to the expected outcomes and then be able to measure against it and tie it to the overall business strategy—which can shorten time to maturity. How will this shortcut time to maturity? By being able to demonstrate the achievement of value across all levels of the hierarchy, you can win over management. If you have management on your side, funding follows. Further, with more influencers convinced of value, politics and culture will be easier to navigate and change, especially for people who don't want to change the way they do things. This is achieved by creating an understanding of the value of change.

As a parallel process, benchmarking usage and adoption on a regular basis will also help demonstrate growth of the program over time as well as help the program determine potential risks or areas of challenge. For example, if you're regularly monitoring application usage by trending the number of users of the system, you can see potential early warning signs. You may notice an area that has onboarded into the program decline in usage. If so, you can drill into the reasons why—and potentially uncover useful feedback before you lose major adoption. This may be the time to pick up the phone; some answers aren't in the data you're looking at.

As maturity evolves in an organization, moving beyond the initial business case for each project and evolving your measures of success to include looking at the total cost of ownership of the program will help in creating the business case for the introduction of standards and the Business Analytics Program team. Often, organizations will be completely focused on costs of an initial investment for technology licenses for a wide group of users due to what might seem like a high initial investment. This may be the most visible and obvious cost, but when you move beyond license cost and delve into the many factors of TCO you will see that typically license cost is only about 20 percent of the equation (Figure 16). The hidden costs of time, resources, and budget spent on hardware, software, consulting, evaluation (including periodic reevaluation of standards), training, internal staffing, marketing, and maintaining vendor relationships are actually the larger expense. By uncovering and communicating this, a Business Analytics Program can quickly show that an initial investment in creating Business Analytics standards and practices for an organization actually decreases overall cost. The costs being spent on hardware, software, support, services, and resource time in duplicate instances around the organization are often not taken into consideration.

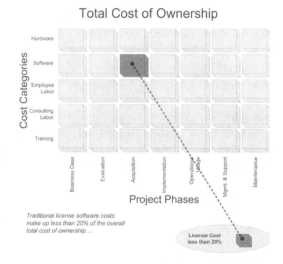

Figure 16: Total Cost of Ownership[4]

As IT efficiency is being increased and the organization enhances its automation capabilities and improves the quality of the information it manages, the efficiencies of the business start to improve as well. Companies start to use the information infrastructure to propel their daily business decisions. Transactions are processed more quickly and more accurately, reducing costly rework and risk to customer satisfaction levels. Business processes are transformed by the ability to enable collaboration between silos.

The value generated is no longer isolated in individual sectors, but is spread across the multiple silos within the organization. The organization begins to understand that individual silos no longer see benefit in isolation, and they integrate into the larger program. The organization may choose a set of standards to reduce the total cost of ownership and will recognize that decision productivity is enhanced through trans-organizational information tools. The enterprise now begins to tap into the archival information from all its subsidiaries and silos to activate its Business Analytics capabilities.

Likewise, as the program evolves and grows, the outcomes of the initial business cases will also begin to be realized. At this time, the program manager will need to create the business value portfolio—a collection of wins that were gained from the program. The full value of each project can now be measured against targets and documented and communicated to the stakeholders. The ability for the organization to move from business strategy to execution and measure success now becomes a simpler task. The discipline of documenting the business case, building the value portfolio, and measuring

KEY CONCEPT

---

[4] John Boyer, Bill Frank, Brian Green, Tracy Harris, and Kay Van De Vanter. *Business Intelligence Strategy: A Practical Guide for Achieving BI Excellence."* Ketchum, ID: MC Press, 2010.

the Business Analytics metrics is not one that happens without focus, but one that must be realized as a key initiative that can shortcut time to maturity and help remove roadblocks that could stall a well-thought-out Business Analytics Program. In the following sections, we go into more detail about these three programmatic exercises. An example of a business value portfolio entry can be found in the "Practical Tips" section of this chapter.

> "Many organizations gear up for the first big win. They show it off and generate a lot of excitement; however, they are not prepared for their own success. They have not planned how to extend this initial success across the organization as a managed program. If they cannot follow up one success with another in a timely manner, the initial excitement dies and so will the overall Business Analytics Program."
>
> —*Kay Van De Vanter*

Step 1: Building a Business Case

The business case is the first step to measuring value because it allows the business owner and analytics team to set goals for the program or project and define the value before they begin. When we speak of a business case, we don't necessarily mean there should be a lengthy, detailed page report prepared before any work is done (a process that would hinder agility and innovation) but to set value targets up front so that all the parties can understand what value they are trying to achieve so the expected outcomes are clear. This will help the team in their understanding of the overall project but will also help to clearly define the focus of the project and requirements. The business case should briefly include:

- Executive summary
  - This is the elevator pitch that briefly conveys the project and benefits.
- Description
  - This section describes the overall project. Include the historical context and how it contributes to the organizational strategy, as well as information that can be used as a benchmark to compare against previous processes and the initial start.
- IT efficiency
  - Outcomes that could be expected (e.g., cost savings related to technology choices, improvements in IT department staff usage).
- Business efficiency
  - Outcomes that are expected (e.g., closing books in two hours rather than five days or automation to make a task less resource intensive, thereby freeing x resources to focus on more strategic tasks).
- Business effectiveness
  - Outcomes that are expected (e.g., how top-level objectives for the organization will be met, business value outcomes such as profit increases through operations visibility, supply chain improvements, customer

satisfaction increases) and how they will be measured. This should extend into IT effectiveness as well.

- Costs
  - ○ Include costs for hardware, software, licenses, maintenance, and so on (typically over three years).
  - ○ People: Provide a high-level estimate (often +/– 50 percent) of resource time required.
- Timeline
  - ○ Provide a high-level timeline in which to expect a return on investment.
- Net value increase total

A business case can be created for both the overall program and for each new major project within the program as they are kicked off. This will set targets and objectives for each project and a way to measure success in the future.

> "Many people mention that they didn't get the ROI they were expecting. When we ask them 'What ROI did you expect?' they respond, 'We didn't define it. We wanted productivity gains, et cetera.' So we must understand that we need to identify outcomes *going into* the project. By doing that, we'll end up with a more focused, streamlined process."
>
> —*Tracy Harris*

Step 2: Building the Value Portfolio

With a business case mindset from the start, building a highly visible set of metrics by which our executives can recognize the ongoing value gets a bit easier. We believe it's extremely important to define, analyze, and document our achievement against goals and continually measure our successes. The analysis of the Business Analytics Program itself is a main function the program owners need to dedicate themselves to.

In our enterprises, priorities change, supportive executives move on, business strategies evolve, and sometimes the perceived value of the Business Analytics Program in the minds of our supporters becomes diluted. After all, how can you sustain the perception of value as the systems, processes, and tools implemented by the Business Analytics Program are incorporated into the business culture? There is the danger that the past successes and accomplishments of the program will fade into the IT infrastructure and end up as something that's recognized only as overhead within the enterprise.

We've spent a considerable amount of time wrestling with the dilemma of demonstrating ongoing value. We've seen that establishing an ecosystem of metrics to measure the program's value not only sustains our executives' interest in the Business Analytics Program but also increases our effectiveness as we sharpen our discipline. We call this the building of the **Business Value Portfolio**. It is an aggregate view of projects and programs managed by the Business Analytics Program. It directly connects to and supports the business strategy by delivering metrics that monitor how those strategies—

technically and contextually—map to the defined goals of management. The purpose of the Business Value Portfolio is to demonstrate the outcomes of the various individual Business Analytics projects in terms of success stories that were achieved. Over time, the Business Value Portfolio provides a great demonstration of the maturity of the program and can help to benchmark how the program has grown and achieved success over time.

The Business Value Portfolio is derived from the business cases but is the measurement of the successes that are seen from the projects. It is a demonstration of where and how BI and Analytics and the processes of the Business Analytics Program are interacting across the enterprise and where there are opportunities for enhancement.

> "What's important to your organization is going to vary. Your standards and what you measure are specific to your organization. How do you claim that analytics has contributed to the value of those things? What happened that wouldn't have happened without this technology or Business Analytics Program? A Business Value Portfolio accumulates its measurements over time. It aggregates them. Then you look at it collectively and you say, 'Wow! There is a lot of business impact.'"
>
> —*Kay Van De Vanter*

The purpose of the Business Value Portfolio is to go back to the initial target to see whether it was achieved after the discrete amount of time and then document it as a success story. This documentation can be in the form of a set of slides that can be downloaded by all the team members in a collaborative area or a series of stories or newsletters and emails that are distributed to the larger team—whichever is best suited to the audience—but keeping track and sharing these wins is a role that needs to be considered so that this documentation occurs. Not only are these activities quantified and monetized by the organization to share the success of the Business Analytics Program, but by creating and managing a Value Portfolio, the program can also uncover or point to areas where improvements can be identified and where streamlining can be effective. The Business Analytics Program must be marketed as much as anything else in the organization that provides business value.

As we've discussed elsewhere, we've found these success stories to be an important part of ongoing adoption to continue the momentum. New project teams gain confidence when they realize that they can build on the successes that preceded them. It creates excitement and momentum, leaving teams feeling enthusiastic about the constant value they are providing.

Step 3: Business Analytics Metrics and Feedback

The value capturing should also include overall Business Analytics metrics and feedback. The tracking of software licenses, reports, user adoption levels, application modifications, and other statistics can be used to build additional understanding of the internal

ROI realized by the organization. These statistics may also offer a view on productivity improvements, reduced processing overheads, poorly utilized or allocated software licenses, and other insights.

By monitoring these metrics with a regular, systematic approach, we can chart the growth of the project and identify where improvements need to be made. Using the historic data as it accumulates, we can spot where certain features or functions of the programs are falling short and identify where we can improve performance through better services, enhanced functions, and stronger information. And, if the business goal is to improve service, reduce costs, or build client loyalty, the supporting analytics captured in this portfolio can help to identify where the ROI resides.

> "It's important to constantly monitor the analytics environment. If we begin to experience response time issues, or if we observe an unexpected decline in activity, then there is something wrong and we need to address it. We measure number of users, activity, throughput, volume of content, et cetera. It's easy to take these metrics for granted, but they are critical."
>
> —*Brian Green*

Usage metrics will help people understand what growth looks like over time and can help teams predict future usage patterns and adoption rates. They will also help teams discover which projects might be falling short of expectations and will help open up the dialogue between teams to understand where improvements might enhance the ability to reach the goals that were set out. These conclusions should be documented and can be included as a section of the Value Portfolio. Using analytics to capture the value of the Business Analytics Program will help strengthen your business case overall.

Another way some of our organizations acquire feedback is through surveys of the customer base that the Business Analytics Program services. Automated technologies can help do this easily today—and in the survey a number of areas can be explored with the teams, from usage to satisfaction to determining what value outcomes have been achieved to date. In addition, using your own analytics on the Business Analytics Program provides another mechanism to demonstrate the capabilities of the analytical tools whose use you are trying to encourage in the organization.

Filling the Value Void

So to recap, why do projects (even programs!) stall, stumble, or fall into irrelevancy? Our experience tells us that they often can falter when the *value* of analytics to the organization's business strategy is uncertain, unclear, undefined, or unmeasured.

Defining the value must not be an afterthought to justify the ROI; it *must* be the rationale for the project initiative. That value should emanate from the top of the organization through the business strategy and cascade down through the organization as the project is defined and analyzed, before the project is formalized.

Then, as business strategies change, organizations grow, and key decision makers move on to new challenges, the past success of any project should be demonstrable to easily remember how its value was defined. And because institutional memory is transient, the key to future success will be the realization that the process of defining value is not an afterthought, but a prerequisite that requires continual monitoring, modification, and maturation.

We feel it's imperative that we devise systems of measurement within the projects of the Business Analytics Program that can readily track, monitor, and demonstrate the value of our projects as a feedback loop to our supporters.

To accomplish these goals, we encourage an upfront business case to be designed to demonstrate the goals of the projects and program—to deliver the key performance indicators that will reflect the successes. By building these metrics into our system—*up front*—we will ensure we can prioritize, repeat our successes, and respond to new challenges with speed and agility and demonstrate the value of the program. In building these metrics, we can then sustain the existing systems, monitor their successes, and continue to fill the Value Void that causes our users confusion and threatens to stall the development of new initiatives in the years to come.

> "Even though we define value up front in our projects, we need the follow-up loop to validate it at the end. . . . If you say you are going to save money, how are you going to measure it, and at what point will you prove out your value? What is the metric? How will it be measured and when? This should be a well-defined step in the project plan."
>
> —*John Boyer*

However, the reason the measurement of value often falls short in a Business Analytics Program is because capturing business value isn't a single monitor of any individual project but a number of metrics and measurements that will be created by different members of the team in IT, finance, or the different business units. It's the upfront definition, overall management, collation, and storage of these that often falls short. Why? Often, it is confusion over whose job it might be—who should fill the role of the great communicator who helps the process become a defined and sustained practice in the organization. However, it is critical to understand that the management of value is what represents how analytics are stimulating the business plan and where opportunities for improvement can be implemented. As goals are achieved, the Business Value Portfolio can demonstrate a lower TCO for the enterprise and an identifiable ROI. In the next part of this chapter, we provide a case study that demonstrates how an organization demonstrated value to grow its Business Analytics program. We will provide a template you can use to begin creating your own business value portfolio plus a checklist to help you measure and demonstrate value. The business value portfolio will help you create the culture and drive the "people" element of the program. This leads us into Chapter 3, where we will dig into the roles, the people, and how to communicate strategy and value to the teams that will drive the analytics culture in your organization.

> **"Don't lose track of the need to quantify business value. Develop this as a discipline so you don't have to backtrack to provide justification."**
>
> *—Brian Green*

Case Study on Value: IBM

From guest author Larry Yarter, Chief Architect,
Business Analytics Center of Competence, IBM

*IBM's focus on value delivers Business Analytics across
IBM's global organization and Business Partner community*

"The key is allowing the business to focus on business problems without
the burden of setting up infrastructure that doesn't add value to the
solution.""

*— Larry Yarter, Chief Architect,
Business Analytics Center of Competence, IBM*

Overview

Blue Insight is IBM's strategic analytics platform, designed to empower hundreds of thousands of IBM employees with access to sophisticated business intelligence and predictive analytics via a cost-effective private cloud architecture. Making this vision a reality involved the usual technical and process issues of centralization, but also social and philosophical ones: How could the Blue Insight team convince users that a centralized private cloud solution was the right way forward for IBM's business to achieve its 2015 roadmap?

Focusing on Value

First launched in 2009, Blue Insight is IBM's strategic analytics initiative, which now delivers Business Analytics across IBM's global organization and Business Partner community. As a centralized service based on a private cloud architecture, Blue Insight is the antithesis of traditional Business Analytics deployments, which are often departmentally based systems designed to address specific needs for individual lines of business. The key to Blue Insight's success is its ability to provide business users with the same flexibility and support for creative analyses, while also releasing massive economies of scale that minimize costs for the business.

Larry Yarter, Chief Architect at Blue Insight's Business Analytics Competency Center (BACC), comments: "In some ways, the technical challenges are the easy part. The advantages of the platform are what help us solve the difficult part, which is to convince all the potential user groups that Blue Insight will give them the same flexibility and enable the same creativity as the departmental business intelligence systems that they have developed for themselves.

"We have been able to show that our strategy is right not only for IBM as a whole but also for each user group individually, because we draw a clear distinction between the well-defined services that we provide and the almost unlimited range of solutions that they can build on top of those services. We contribute the infrastructure, the software, and the service level guarantees; they provide the data and the creative analyses that enable them to gain insight from it. Effectively, they still get all the flexibility of building their own solution, but we can give them the commodity services faster, more reliably, and at a cost of around 20 cents on the dollar. The key is allowing the business to focus on business problems without the burden of setting up infrastructure that doesn't add value to the solution."

IBM Best Practices in Delivering Value

The success of the program is based on increasing user adoption and delivering value across all areas of the business value hierarchy. Some best practices include:

✓ *Start with high-value initial wins with champions and grow:* To drive adoption of the new platform, the BACC team initially focused on bringing on board projects that could demonstrate high levels of value with users who were enthusiastic about the prospect of analytics and who could champion their success. With the success of these initial projects, word spread across IBM about the value that Blue Insight could deliver, and increasing numbers of user groups began asking to join the initiative.

✓ *Engage executive levels:* At the same time, high-level support from IBM's senior executives made a significant contribution to raising awareness of the strategic intent and persuading different parts of the business to move from their existing platforms. The executive team supplied communications resources to get the message out across IBM's entire worldwide, multi-brand, multi-channel business.

✓ *Engage business and IT in partnership:* By culturally and organizationally working together and defining the role of each team in the partnership, success was achieved that produced outstanding results.

Reaping the Benefits

As departments have moved onto Blue Insight, they have begun to decommission their old analytics systems, which is projected to save approximately $25 million over five years through reduced hardware, software, facilities, and human resources costs. Equally, for teams that did not have an analytics solution before they adopted Blue Insight, there are significant benefits in terms of cost avoidance.

"If you go about it the traditional way, setting up an infrastructure to deliver analytics services as part of each project is a complex task," explains Larry Yarter. "You have to get budget approval, purchase servers, find space for them in a data center, and power, cool, and maintain them. And that's before you even think about the software. On average it takes about six months and $250,000 to get a new analytics environment up and running with development, test, and production environments. With our private cloud architecture, we can generally deploy solutions in a couple of days, and at about 10 percent of that cost."

In the long term, the real value of Blue Insight for IBM will be the insight it offers into the company's operations, which provides a basis for better decision making and improved performance and efficiency.

One impressive example is a project that uses Blue Insight to analyze small deals management within IBM Software Group. By analyzing data on potential sales opportunities, IBM is able to improve the efficiency of its allocation of leads to sales channels. Smaller deals are passed on to IBM Business Partners who have the relevant skills and resources to close the deals, enabling IBM's own sales teams to focus on enterprise-level clients. As a result of this more-effective use of sales resources, Software Group has seen an 8 percent increase in small deals revenue—making a major contribution to IBM's 2015 growth targets.

Proven Business Benefits

Business area	Benefits	Business impact
Small deals management	Allocating leads to sales channels more effectively	8% increase in revenue
IT and business	Eliminating and reducing tools, hardware, software and HR costs	$25M USD
Various business areas	Cost avoidance by adopting Blue Insight instead of building a departmental solution	$250,000 per project
IT	Time saved in getting new users up and running on a new analytics initiative	Days instead of months

Since 2009, the Blue Insight program has grown to support nearly 200,000 users across 390 projects and draws data from over 250 source systems. The program delivered 1.7 million reports In Q3 2011, and it draws from 250 data sources across various operating systems and hardware platforms with a small operations team of nine BACC support staff and 10 infrastructure staff. The business benefits across the various lines of business are being realized each and every day with new projects onboarding and delivering value.

Practical Tips for Measuring and Demonstrating Value: Creating the Business Value Portfolio

In the Value chapter, we discussed creating a Business Value Portfolio—a dynamic document that will track and measure value for each project that is managed by the Business Analytics Program. The Business Value Portfolio will grow over time with each win in the series of successful projects that are undertaken by the Business Analytics Program. Various methods can be used to collect this information:

- Interviews with team members and business owners
- Surveys to project teams at various stages of the project
- Measurements with the Business Analytics tools ("Business Analytics on Business Analytics")

Below is a sample template that can be used for each project undertaken by the program. Information should be captured in advance to understand the program's expected value and then again at different points throughout the project.

Sample Business Value Portfolio Template*

Title: Example: *Sales team increases visibility to improve revenue outcome.*

Project Team: List business owners, analytic team members, and IT teams.

Business Problem: State, in business terms, the business problem that needed to be solved. Example: *The sales team had little visibility into current pipeline, resulting in slow reaction time to potential gaps.*

Value Outcomes Expected: Detail specific business effectiveness outcomes. Example: *By increasing visibility, the sales teams felt that they could improve sales by x%, resulting in X more revenue.*

Current Process: Provide detail about the existing process that was being used. Example: *The sales team was using spreadsheets, which they were filling out and sending to a central point in the organization. Detail what the downfalls of this process were and why it needed to be adjusted.*

Improvements Made: Provide information about the solution that was implemented and how the process was changed.

Benefits Received: Detail specific business effectiveness outcomes achieved to date. Example: *Increased revenue, customer satisfaction, public outcomes, expense, or asset management.*

Detail specific business efficiency outcomes achieved to date. Example: *Faster processes, time to results, increased productivity, internal satisfaction.*

Detail specific IT efficiencies achieved to date. Example: *Improved total cost of ownership (by how much?); management, maintenance, and administration gains; expense reduction in IT.*

Benchmark Data: Provide any benchmark data that has been taken over time that shows growth of analytics adoption, including number of users, number of reports, and amount of data being consumed.

Next Steps for the Project: Detail any future steps, enhancements, or follow-on projects that will be done.

*Note: Insert quotes throughout the portfolio entry from members of the team and business owners.

Practical Tips

- The goal of this effort is not to create long case studies, but a story that can be captured in roughly a page.
- Creating a slide presentation from the captured details, plus pictures of the completed work and photos of team members, and showing the presentation at community meetings is a great way to promote engagement.
- Housing these stories on an intranet area where they can be accessed and updated is useful.
- Surveying business owners every few months can help to measure continual value.

Value Checklist

The Value chapter discussed a number of program areas that should be considered for your Business Analytics Program to measure and demonstrate value. Use this checklist to see which areas might be useful to integrate and manage over time in your organization:

- ✓ Has someone on your team been identified to continually measure and report on the value of projects?
- ✓ Do you have knowledge of the tools in your organization that can be used to collect this data (surveys, templates)?
- ✓ Do you create a business case when embarking on a new project to understand the value up front?
- ✓ Are you capturing the business effectiveness expected outcomes and measuring against them?
- ✓ Are you capturing the business efficiency expected outcomes and measuring against them?
- ✓ Are you capturing the IT efficiency expected outcomes and measuring against them?
- ✓ Are you capturing benchmarks over time that can demonstrate value?
- ✓ Are you maintaining a Business Value Portfolio?
- ✓ Are you demonstrating and sharing these successes with the team to aid understanding of the program's value across the organization?

Chapter 3
Key #3: People

In the first two chapters, we discussed how you can manage a changing strategy and prioritize analytics initiatives against demonstrable and measurable value. To execute on your plans, a key factor is having the right people on board and understanding their role in the program. A Business Analytics Program will utilize a wide range of skills throughout the organization, but getting the right people on board and building the organizational support for their skills can be challenging. At the same time, gaining the momentum required for a Business Analytics Program requires an understanding of the larger corporate organization: its culture, its politics, and the relationships of the crucial management roles and stakeholders within the organization. Finally, having the critical management support for the Business Analytics Program will require levels of communication and *evangelism* for Business Analytics processes that will propel the program across the organizational culture itself. At the root of this is change—which is always difficult—and managing these changes in a way that engages the broader team.

> "Because there are so many variables, you need to be creative in addressing the organizational challenges. It is intellectually challenging, much like chess where no two games are alike. The only problem is that chess is just a game, but this is real life with real consequences."
>
> —John Boyer

So, who are the right people? What kinds of skills are required? What roles will they play? How will you attract them and sustain them in their activities? How do you drive an analytics culture and bring team members on board to engage in the process and possibly engage in transformational change?

> "People. . . . A Business Analytics Program in many ways would be a lot easier if it weren't for people."
>
> —Bill Frank

In this chapter, we discuss a few areas that will increase your success, and we discuss some of the challenges you can avoid with the "People" element of the initiative through:

- Understanding the maturity of the organization and its analytic culture
- Managing ongoing executive involvement
- Building your organizational design— the Analytics Center of Excellence
- Identifying skills, talent, and roles
- Managing relationships, communication, and evangelism

> "Technology, for the most part, is actually the easy part of the equation. It's people that are the challenge."
>
> —*John Boyer*

We believe that the people element of the program is where you will face the biggest risk of derailment if this element is not managed well. Organizational design alone has been known to create political issues. The value of the program must be understood at the highest levels. By making sure that the people element of the program is a top priority, Business Analytics Programs can ensure a speedier route to success and maintain momentum over time.

Maturity of the Business Analytics Program

Most of us have gone through the startup phases of our Business Analytics project and/or program, and we've also interviewed many other leaders in this space. Except in those organizations where the Business Analytics Programs were created by new management, almost all have begun the evolution of their organizational design as small teams that started by addressing specific challenges faced by their sponsoring organizations. These challenges could be licensing or infrastructure, a specific business application, a resource pool, training program, or other issue. If we consider the AQ Maturity Model as the frame for the evolution of the organizational design and culture in an organization, Figure 17 depicts a potential makeup of a typical early-stage program.

The basic configuration of an early-stage program often consists of project or business leaders who rely on both a technical (IT) expert and a skilled business analyst. The level of collaboration is usually multidimensional across roles, building to the goals set by the sponsoring entity. Often, it is a virtual team established on trust or like-minded individuals who understand what they can achieve. This configuration often will present a high-collaboration environment with like-minded, cross-functional team members working together toward a common goal.

But as the Business Analytics Program progresses and success grows, other team members may gradually be brought into the fold. Collaboration across departments and silos within the organization is a valuable element in this evolution, but one that is hard

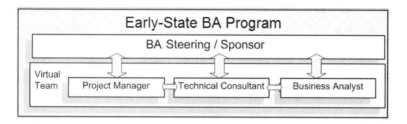

Figure 17: Early-Stage BA Program

to maintain as Business Analytics skills grow in the organization. There may be different evolutions of this design, where a Business Analytics Competency Center may emerge in the IT or Information Management department on their own strategic objective. There also may be line-of-business teams that operate independently or create their own Center of Excellence. In most cases, this may happen simultaneously where multiple silos of initiatives exist—with some loosely connected and others on renegade and independent paths. The environment may appear chaotic with various political undertones. This situation may continue for a considerable amount of time, until a champion and executive leader looks closely at the design and determines a more strategic path that leverages skills in a way that reduces total cost of ownership and raises business effectiveness through better teaming, collaboration, and integration. This step may be the result of a larger event—a failure to achieve business targets, a new executive joining the team, or a vision event that defines the challenges and needs, for example.

However, as an analytics champion, you can demonstrate how the time to success can be shortened. Understanding that early teaming can reduce cost and time for the organization and lessen politics and knowing the steps involved to bring these silos together can move the various teams in lock-step with one another. It is important, at these developmental stages, not to boil the ocean from the outset but to keep the goals of the target Business Analytics project well-defined in a roadmap of steps. Many successful BA Programs began with a scaled-back set of goals and then built on their achievements to the next set of challenges. They started small, examined their domains for strategic values that could be attained, and then acted incrementally to arrive at the prescribed destination, enlisting teams as the program grew.

Scope creep and lack of agility are common challenges for these burgeoning teams. For instance, as a particular project starts to achieve success, it's usual for that success to inspire other departments to pile on requirements for new reports, slowing development and expanding expectations. The team in place may not keep up with demand and, instead of empowering others, may put more rigid processes in place. This occurrence might result in a loss of trust, excessive layers of bureaucracy, and people going back to their old ways, creating silos and independent solutions. One excellent technique to manage these challenges is to develop roadmaps with the stakeholders and enablement plans so that management sponsors can begin to envision the overall potential and scale or manage expectations. The roadmaps address those future requirements in "waves," identifying when particular business areas will be brought in based on priority or when technology features will be implemented. Through this incremental approach, goals can be achieved in a more controlled and scalable manner. Each success will then lay the framework for the next project.

> "In the earliest stages of a Business Analytics Program, define some milestones that are attributable more to the engagement process itself. The reality is that data quality may be poor and requirements will need to change repeatedly. Along the way, claim the victories that are evident from engaging with users, discovering business requirements, and enabling the development of solutions."
>
> —*Brian Green*

What we've seen, using this incremental approach, is a recognizable pattern or structure that gradually emerges. In some organizations, team membership will rotate as certain elements take shape. In others, some "fixed" or semi-permanent positions are created. Individual teams working on individual Business Analytics projects may converge into a single entity or department. The team will evolve as the program grows—both the fixed Business Analytics department and the various line-of-business areas that may manage their own initiatives. A central team—perhaps with the Chief Analytics Officer and Center of Excellence—that is responsible for program management, onboarding, and communication is necessary, as is an infrastructure team that will manage technology, standards, and support. However, convergence of these teams can increase the collaboration and centralize the expertise needed to meet the strategic goals of the organization. You will see these structures in many forms, and they might be called a Business Intelligence Competency Center (BICC), an Analytics Center of Excellence, a Business Analytics Community of Practice, or another similar name.

Most successful Business Analytics Programs have an identified structure in some shape or form. For example, the expertise of a database administrator may become a central requirement to coordinate the information. Or, teams may remain "virtual," composed of members from a variety of departments. The membership of the team may rotate in a line-of-business expert with specific knowledge of a particular process. But the essential thing to remember is that each Business Analytics Program's growth uniquely represents the organization's needs, its aspirations, and its cultural values interfacing with the appropriate talents that are available.

Mature Business Analytics Programs

> "As part of your Business Analytics Program, you need to plan for your success. This includes expanding not only infrastructure but also processes, policies, licenses, and people. When your program begins, it may be small, and the need to have specific policies, people, and processes in place may not be obvious. As you grow, you will soon find that you will need to grow in other ways that are essential to the health of the program."
>
> —*Kay Van De Vanter*

Some equate this evolutionary process with the *maturity level* of the individual Business Analytics Program, but it also needs to be recognized as a reflection of the enterprise's business culture. However, mature programs can be characterized by:

- An Executive Steering Committee that is active, involved, and able to establish and support priorities.
- An organization assessed broadly for readiness. Cultural competency, technical capabilities, and understanding of Business Analytics are measured and remediation or educational programs have established standards defined around people, process, and technologies.
- Standards adopted for people, process, and technology throughout the organization in both business and IT.
- Fixed team members with strong program management skills to communicate, coordinate, and collaborate.
- Empowerment of individuals with analytic skills in various business domain areas.
- Strong IT collaboration and participation driven by meeting the needs of the business.
- Finance involvement that is in lock-step with line-of-business and IT strategies.

Some mature organizations may have various Centers of Excellence in the different business departments or domain areas of the business to ensure business expertise is applied to the program while having a team to manage infrastructure and standards; however, the program and strategy team itself needs to bind the teams together in collaboration as a community. In other mature organizations, these skilled business experts sit directly in the Business Analytics department to interface out with the business teams as the bridge. Either approach can be successful, but success will depend on the structure, culture, and organization of the larger organization and having the right mix of people, process, and technology elements in place.

Executive Involvement

Mature business analytics programs tend to have high executive involvement. When we discuss "executive involvement," we mean both the top executive responsible for the Business Analytics Program success—such as a CIO, CFO, CEO, or potentially a Chief Analytics Officer—but also the key executives who manage the various points of the business strategy.

Why is widespread executive support so important? Executive support for the Business Analytics Program is more than just approval for individual Business Analytics projects. It is a key element that keeps the focus on the larger strategic vision of the Business Analytics in the organization, informing participants on the program goals, creating the culture of performance, and communicating the value of analytics across the breadth of the organization.

Obtaining, growing, and sustaining the attention of the executive team and their recognition of the strategic value of the Business Analytics Program can often be difficult when the executive may be struggling with its own priorities. Keeping and building further executive support is an ongoing job—one that needs to be a consistent part of program management. Let's discuss how to do this.

Gaining Ongoing Support

Executives will have clear direction on the goals they are trying to achieve, but those not directly accountable for Business Analytics Program success may not be looking to Business Analytics as the method by which they can gather insight about, support, and measure these goals that will contribute to their achievement. Therefore, engaging each executive role in the organization may demand a different focus, language, and communication of how priorities can be achieved with the right mix of technology (tools and data), processes, and people at their fingertips.

As an example, a CEO's top priorities may include setting the strategic direction and articulating the corporate vision. This leader must ensure business goals are met in a timely and cost-effective way. This is a substantially more comprehensive role than that of the CIO, whose typical primary priorities might be enabling business innovation, improving customer satisfaction, reducing costs, and creating competitive advantage. Meanwhile, the CFO may be focused on yet entirely different priorities, such as measuring and monitoring business performance, meeting the company's fiduciary and regulatory requirements, and monitoring process and business improvement. Finally, a line-of-business executive may typically be focused on driving day-to-day operational performance to improve profits, increase productivity, and reduce business risk. Each executive role is highly nuanced toward the immediate problems at hand while attempting to meet the specific requirements dictated by the current business climate and laddering up to the corporate strategy.

Learning these executives' priorities and the language they use in their roles—as well as the responsibilities that come with their jobs—offers you the opportunity to apply your understanding of Business Analytics to their business problems and help them to address their practical difficulties while working toward the organization's strategic goals.

However, some Business Analytics Programs have been tempted to approach all senior executives with the same business message. This practice often results in less understanding about how each particular area or responsibility can benefit from the Business Analytics outcomes. How can these individual messages be adapted? Of course, each organization is different; nonetheless, several important lessons have been learned during the ongoing enlistment processes of top executives in our organizations:

- **Know your audience**. Start with a "laser focus" on their pain and then expand. What executive won't stop to listen to you if you tell them you know how they can reach their top-level target to grow the business by *x* percent in growth markets, cut the time-to-delivery and costs for their products, or manage expenses by 10 percent without losing valuable staff? Know their individual pain points *before* approaching the various stakeholders, and develop a strategy for how the Business Analytics Program can alleviate those problems. Then help them understand how working together—and with other departments and technologies—will benefit their overall business and why.
- **Talk the talk.** Speak the language of the individual or business area to demonstrate how the specific *value* of the Business Analytics Program can help in their areas. Communicate in business-specific, nontechnical terms. The business people understand the outcomes they are trying to achieve in their specific areas of the business. When discussing technology, many individuals may relate better to "data" than to "data models," to "information" vs. "Information Management," or to "drill" and "slice" vs. "OLAP."
- **Demonstrate value.** Document results and proof points. Stress the positive wins your Business Analytics projects have already accomplished so that your wider audiences can see the effectiveness of your strategic thinking. Pull from your Business Value Portfolio some high-level, quantifiable results and references from business partners. It may also be appropriate to point to external references that demonstrate the point.
- **Talk results.** The conversation should start with asking for the executives' support but should be framed with a high-level benefit. Executives are generally eager to obtain funding for projects once they understand the results that can be achieved. If you can improve revenue, increase customer satisfaction, or cut expenses in a way that will offset any cost that is being requested, an executive will be much more receptive to the budget component. While there may be a tendency to focus on reducing cost or increasing revenue, intangible benefits, such as work/life balance, productivity, or even access to data that was previously hard to obtain or analyze, may also be something an executive supports.

- **Keep them informed.** Start small, and stress incremental progress toward *their* goals. Don't get caught just in talking to your goals or a larger strategic initiative; make sure they understand regularly how their goals are being met. Show value as soon as possible, and, if necessary, get the executive to help you "bend the rules" in an ethical and compliant way (e.g., expediting a process). Keep the communication flowing.
- **Refine the elevator pitch.** Gain executives' trust and respect their time by being well-organized and ready with a list of results aimed at their areas of responsibility. Regular updates in a very short time frame will be highly appreciated. Squeeze in 15 minutes to provide a quick, results-oriented update, and over time you will see that the door will be open for much longer periods because you respected their time and provided what they wanted to hear. Use whatever communication methods fit your organization's culture.
- **Close the loop.** Maintain contact, and continually circle back with measurements and results achieved. Asking for support and resources and then never closing the loop with outcomes will result in a loss of trust and potentially cause the executives to forget the reason they were inspired in the first place.

Remember that gaining executive support for the Business Analytics Program won't be the end of Business Analytics journey; it's only the beginning of a longer-term conversation. Executive support isn't a blank check, but an ongoing task. It's your responsibility to monitor the progress of their support and to keep the conversations with the executives in gear on an ongoing basis. Factor this into Business Analytics Program time and into the type of skills and talent required to fill this role. If you keep a Business Value Portfolio and regularly monitor the success achieved by the program, this task can be much easier to undertake over time.

Conversation Starters

If you're having trouble setting up that meeting with the executive three levels up, see whether one of these approaches will get his or her attention and get you in the door:

"I'm writing our Business Analytics Strategy; could I interview you? I'd love to understand your vision for this company."

"Did you hear that one of our projects boosted profits 300 percent last year through the use of Business Analytics"?

"I understand some of your staff are struggling with (choose one) finding the information they need; meeting deadlines to provide mandatory reports; crunching data with outdated desktop tools. I'd like to suggest some ways we can help."

Organizational Design:
The Analytics Center of Excellence

The organizational designs that exist can be found with various names:

- Business Intelligence Competency Center
- Analytics Center of Excellence
- Business Intelligence Community of Practice
- Analytics Department
- Branded internal names such as "DecisionOne Team," "ImpactCentral," or other innovative names

Regardless of the name, a defined organizational design is necessary. In this book, we choose to call this the Analytics Center of Excellence. Many IT teams opt to call the infrastructure and technical team of experts a Competency Center, but we include the community of lines of business, the strategy office, and the IT team in our definition. We also felt it could be called a "community" because each design tends to have analytic expertise and interest inside and outside a single, structured group, but we concluded that "community" as a term is a bit looser than we recommend and does not quite well enough provide the understanding of strong relationships, role definitions, and defined responsibilities that need to be undertaken.

Most of these initiatives start small and grow the team over time. When we talk about growing the team, this also may not always be in the structured, centralized Business Analytics core team—but in all the business areas that surround it. For Business Analytics initiatives to become strategic, they will still require input and interaction that is much broader in scope than the average IT project. They will also demand early buy-in and collaboration between multiple business and IT entities across the organization. This is especially true of senior management, plus the in-depth support from each of the organization's key decision-making areas.

Organizational design is not to be taken lightly. Defined roles, responsibility, and mandated communication between teams is necessary to move a larger team into a collaborative state. Also, as the program grows and changes, management teams can address the future of the program with better acuity.

Samples of Analytics Center of Excellence designs can be found in the "Practical Tips" section at the end of this chapter. Regardless of the design, each will work well as long as the right resources, role definitions, skills, and expertise are in place to either manage or interface with the partners that need to be engaged and as long as dedicated communication is present from the executive level through to the working team members. This design will also have to change frequently, stakeholders will need to be brought into the fold, and cross-team program management will become a greater task.

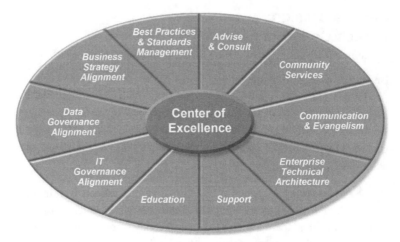

Figure 18: Center of Excellence Focus Areas[1]

Roles and responsibilities within the Program could exist within the Strategy Center of the Analytics Center of Excellence, within associated IT teams, or in the Centers of Excellence located in the business. In Figure 18, you can see the typical focus areas that need to be considered over time for the Center of Excellence.

While these are the most common areas that need to be defined, a Business Analytics Program and Center of Excellence might not support all of them in the beginning—but might rather grow the support for these areas across functions over time to scale the effort broadly. The Center of Excellence Team—in its definition of the scope and the role—will also have to create a charter and vision for the teams to ensure there is a clear understanding of responsibility. Defining which teams and members are responsible for the various functions is key to the growth and success of the program. Let's discuss what each of these roles might contain:

- **Business Strategy Alignment:** Responsible for cross-team collaboration in creation of the strategy, mapping corporate priorities, value, and objectives to create a roadmap and direction for the program—including understanding of the organizational design, mapping capabilities to user needs, and evolving the strategy over time. Create the business case, apply value, and manage the overall program.

[1] John Boyer, Bill Frank, Brian Green, Tracy Harris, and Kay Van De Vanter. *Business Intelligence Strategy: A Practical Guide for Achieving BI Excellence.* Ketchum, ID: MC Press, 2010.

- **Best Practices and Standards Management:** Ensuring that standard technologies that meet the strategic needs of the organization and best practices are shared to accelerate and balance time-to-value with consistency and cost management.
- **Advise and Consult:** Enablement and best practice sharing, delivery of expertise to empower new users and teams, and internal "consulting" teams that enable self-sufficiency.
- **Community Services:** Build "gold standard" reports, rules, or metrics that the broader team can use, and provide a skilled team that can be leveraged for key projects, upstarts, and defining standard frameworks.
- **Communication and Evangelism:** Responsible for communication, showcasing, and other forms of cross-team collaboration that align teams to a common goal. Assists with program management aspects and keeping the community aligned, informed, and driving the analytics culture.
- **Enterprise Technical Architecture:** Envision, direct, build, and support the technical infrastructure. This may include an innovation team that can test and introduce new capabilities to the program.
- **Education and Support:** Train and support the broad user base, and design the right level of training for the right users. These team members would be the internal first point of contact for support issues or help required.
- **IT Governance Alignment:** These members would interface or work with the broader IT governance processes and can include areas such as project and change management, portfolio management, vendor management, and license management.
- **Data Governance Alignment:** This team function is responsible for the intersection with the data governance processes across the organization.

Whether these functions are managed within a central, structured team or are managed virtually through different teams but brought together as a Community within the Center of Excellence structure is based on maturity and structure of the overall organization itself—but clear role definition and responsibility are the keys to making it work.

Organizational Design and Program Funding Models

As services become increasingly shared, or as teams converge, the organization will need to formulate the most effective means of funding and sponsoring the Business Analytics Program. Without a defined organizational design, there is a temptation by management to treat the Business Analytics Program as an ad hoc task force that is subject to the political and cultural climate of the immediate business situation. Larger strategic business goals become confused with urgent needs or associated with individual supporters whose roles within the organization are changing. Therefore, establishing clear roles and a design that will demonstrate the strategic means by which the business can improve performance can deliver new meaning to the program or department and increased value to the program itself. This may change the funding model over time as the program matures. We typically have seen three models emerge as a program matures over time:

- Self-funded projects
- Shared Service Chargeback Model
- Centrally Funded Service

Early-stage programs are often funded as point projects to solve a particular business need. This is a great way to get the program off the ground and prove success. As the program grows, it may be funded via a single department that recuperates cost as a chargeback. This is where a single department such as IT may take on the initial funding but charge back for consulting, design, R&D, education, services, or hosting to the various teams that use the program services or technologies. However, while this model may easily enlist the pioneers and forward-thinkers, it will likely not encourage the departments that are lagging or entering into their own initiatives. Therefore, as the program becomes more strategic and gains momentum, it typically becomes a program that is funded across programs or, ideally, funded from the top, enabling users across the business to enlist into the program "free of charge" to overcome objections and maintain standard technologies, encouraging broader adoption. We recommend moving toward the funding model that is undertaken as a larger infrastructure cost—the Centrally Funded Service rather than a chargeback—to not limit adoption. Once team members reach a barrier of cost, the team may decide to seek its own solutions. Centrally Funded Services tend to gain higher user adoption and less risk of fragmentation.

KEY CONCEPT

Skills, Talents, and Roles

So who should be involved in the Business Analytics Program? What kinds of skills and talents are needed? How are the roles identified and managed? In today's environment, there are more analytic requests than skills in the industry. This means that in many organizations, careful pairing of business skills and IT skills might be necessary. In this section, we provide an overview of the most common roles and skills required.

We feel that there are three main groups of skills required: business and program skills, analytical skills, and IT infrastructure skills. In the following paragraphs, we discuss the types of roles and skills that should be considered as the program develops.

Chief Analytics Officer

This is a fairly new role that is just starting to emerge—one that we believe could be a valuable asset to any organization. The Chief Analytics Officer is the top executive responsible for Business Analytics Strategy in an organization. This person is responsible for working across the executive set, prioritizing strategies, creating roadmaps, defining capabilities required, managing the program, and guiding the overall Analytics Center of Excellence. He or she works closely with the CIO, CFO, CMO, and lines of business, as well as the CEO, to ensure priorities are met and cross-team collaboration is strong. This role could report into various teams in a dotted-line fashion.

Business Analytics Steering Committee

A spearheading role involves the personnel who make up the Business Analytics Steering Committee. We firmly believe that the committee should be made up of management or nominated members who are elected by the management team to represent the executive stakeholder who is a senior leader in the team. In addition, we see the importance of having representatives from both IT and the business areas of the company. That's because the purpose of the Business Analytics Steering Committee is to establish and maintain the strategic vision of the program, prioritize strategic initiatives, and be key decision makers during the evolution—enforcing established standards, funding mechanisms, and clear prioritization. Committee members should be key decision makers with broad knowledge of their domain area, influence, and decision-making ability.

Line-of-Business or Domain Experts

Individuals who can act as the representatives from lines of business that drive the business needs are important to provide the project with the detailed requirements, measurements, and domain area expertise that will result in successful outcomes. Line-of-Business Experts may work in collaboration with Analytic Experts if they do not possess analytic technical skills; however, they should be knowledgeable about available data, metrics, measurements, and business goal design. They will have deep expertise in the line of business or domain area and will hold influential roles, regarded as experts that are trusted by the business area. They will be charged with the execution of the business requirements of each project.

Analytic Experts

BI specialists, statisticians, predictive analysts, data scientists, data engineers, business analysts, and financial analysts are exceptionally important in sorting through the scope of information that's emanating from the vast array of sources. These individuals are experts in their analytic field and may be Line-of-Business or Domain Experts as well—but they can turn data into metrics, plans, budgets, predictions, forecasts, statistics, or the output that is required to strategically gain insight into the business needs.

A very important skill that needs to be sought from the roles is the "storyteller" role. Not only is it important to understand what to look for in the data, but to weave it into a cohesive story—one that can provide solutions to the executive team, managers, and decision makers who need the information. These roles are most valuable when the Analytic Expert, who can use the technology, is also the Line-of-Business expert; however, in today's world, individuals with both deep technical and business skills are in short supply.

In the absence of an Analytic Expert who is a business expert, pairing the Line-of-Business or Domain Expert with the Analytic Expert that has the right technology skill set can achieve the same objective. However, each of these different types of analytic roles requires different skill sets, training, and educational knowledge. A BI specialist may not have the same expertise as the data scientist, nor the financial forecaster. Therefore, understanding the various capabilities required and ensuring the right skills are hired—and kept current in their training—is a key to success.

Business Analytic Program Expert

Program Experts will be providing all the roles of Business Analytics Program strategy, direction, management, program development, support, communication, and evangelism. This role should be part of the Analytics Center of Excellence, and will be the Business Analytics *Champion*. Those in this role should have a strong Business Analytics background combined with program management skills, management and leadership skills, and, potentially, marketing or sales experience to help communicate and enlist team members and manage communities. Training experts may also be enlisted as part of the program role.

Information Management and DBA Roles

There's a need for skilled Information Management professionals, such as database administrators (DBAs), data integration and governance experts, compliance analysts, BI architects, data architects, and many other Information Management roles to support the Business Analytics Program. These roles maintain the consistency of the information as it's pulled from numerous data sources, put the data into business models, create taxonomies, develop semantic layers, and monitor how those data sources change over the life of each project as other IT development projects evolve.

For instance, organizations often start with line-of-business systems (transactional systems) that feed off of multiple databases to deliver the initial business reports that users are requesting. These reports—which support the organization in the initial phases of a Business Analytics practice—can sometimes result in conflicting information developed from other transactional systems. The challenge for DBAs is to analyze the data emanating from the various transactional databases and to transform the data into a comprehensive data warehouse where appropriate for use by the entire organization.

Systems and Support Team

The Systems and Support Team establishes, tests, supports, and maintains the hardware and software infrastructure that supports the entire Business Analytics Program community. These individuals will provide expertise for performance tuning, system monitoring, expanding hardware or software capabilities to ensure the infrastructure is achieving optimal performance and supporting the onboarding of the team, scaling the infrastructure, and analyzing needs as it grows. These are the technology specialists who know the infrastructure and will continue to maintain it on a day-to-day basis. This is also the set of technology professionals who can test, troubleshoot and solve technical issues to support the teams in their continued business needs.

Graphic Design, Usability, and Visualization

How information is visualized, how easy it is to understand it at a glance, and how well-designed and appealing it is has become critical to Business Analytics teams. In many cases, it may be fairly easy to put together a beautiful dashboard—but is it conveying the information in the most appropriate way? Can less-skilled consumers use the analytics provided? Are the provided analytics graphically pleasing enough to engage the user? Graphic design and usability specialists are increasingly joining the Business Analytics teams to deliver concise, easy-to-understand, and graphically pleasing outputs to ensure critical information can be easily shared and disseminated. These specialists need to be included as part of the analytics team—whether as full-time, part-time, or virtual members—and must have a good understanding of the tools and technologies to provide guidance on the user interface as well as the dashboard design.

Offshore or Outsource?

First of all, these two options are not the same. Some companies outsource certain business functions to vendors that specialize in those areas; payroll processing and management consulting are common examples of this practice. Other companies choose to "offshore" specific processes or services; the help desk call center is one ubiquitous example. The discussion gets complicated because many outsourcing companies now offshore their services and deliver them to their clients transparently.

Although differences exist between the two, both involve moving processes or services outside the borders of either the company (outsource) or the country (offshore). The motivation for the conversations nearly always arises out of a desire to save money through lower costs or increased efficiencies. Like the general marketplace, we have not come to a consensus on the best practices. Most of our companies have tried one or both with mixed success.

- While the motivation is usually cost savings, do not focus on a single metric. For example, just because hourly rates may be cheaper offshore, there is rarely a one-for-one replacement of in-house expertise.
- When considering either offshoring or outsourcing, ask, "Is this a core part of our business, or is it a support or administrative function?" Support or administration may be moved outside with less disruption to the business or customers, whereas it is difficult to farm out your expertise—what your business is known for.
- The decision may depend on the size of your company. For some smaller companies, one of these options may extend your reach or capabilities.
- Do not neglect to consider the cultural impact on your company. Offshoring, perhaps more so than outsourcing, is an organizational change. Your staff may need to learn a new culture, accommodate new business hours, and establish new processes.

- It can be emotional. Just as when robots were first introduced to manufacturing, many employees fear the changes that come with offshoring and outsourcing, sometimes due to xenophobia or personal insecurities. Over-communicate, and deal proactively with the people issues.
- However much planning you put into the decision, there will be an adjustment period. There will be a learning curve on both sides. There will need to be changes in responsibilities.
- Consider adopting technologies to facilitate remote meetings and collaboration.

Best practices in offshoring or outsourcing analytics are still currently in development. This path may be an option, but choose the elements wisely. We typically recommend that new and innovative projects that are undergoing change should keep analytic experts and business specialists in close proximity to one another to allow iterative design, develop the relationship for innovation, and create momentum. At times, this may require the help of outsource experts; however, close and constant communication is necessary.

How Many Team Members Should Be in a Center of Excellence?

The next question that is typically asked about the Center of Excellence is how many team members a Center of Excellence should contain. We feel this question is irrelevant—a Center of Excellence will grow and change over time. It depends on organizational culture and design as well as maturity, which means this number can vary. Organizational designs that are much more centralized may have a large number of people who work within a structured team and are shared as analytic experts in an organization, while others may have analytic experts in the lines of business that interface with structured infrastructure and program management teams. The goal of the Center of Excellence is to enable users throughout the business to be empowered to self-serve, to develop an analytic culture, and to create pervasive use. Therefore, this might essentially mean that the end goal is to have an overall organization that uses analytics broadly and therefore has a very large community that supports and uses analytics.

Whether some of these roles are part of the Center of Excellence or whether they interface as-needed from their own teams can be based on maturity and overall organizational design, but understanding the needed skills and finding the necessary talent is an important element of success. If the required skills fall outside the structured team, the relationship management and program management elements become even more critical to the program. This will help to enlist the talent needed and drive an analytic culture that will create passionate team members and collaboration.

In the next section, we discuss the elements of relationship management, its importance, and tips on how to drive an analytic culture that will encourage collaboration, communication, and accelerate success.

Relationship Management, Communication, and Evangelism: Developing the Culture of Analytics

It's not enough to merely build a technically proficient Business Analytics Program, or to successfully acquire ongoing executive support. Business climates change, disruptive technologies can sideline technical investments and delay organizational goals, and individual executive sponsors can move on to new challenges. Without an active strategy for managing your Business Analytics Program's relationships with others, there is always the threat that its goals and its visibility within the organization may falter. We've found it's essential to ensure that the technology is accepted and used effectively, and this requires that the Business Analytics Program identify best practices and develop guidelines for successful implementation of Business Analytics tools.

The Elements of Relationship Management Success

We believe there are seven crucial elements that can speed the acceptance of the Analytics Program and benefit the organization as a whole:

- Creating technology standards
- Managing the Business Analytics product standards
- Onboarding and enabling the larger team
- Creating a culture and encouraging collaboration
- Establishing timely, trusted information
- Building the communication strategy
- Training your users

Create Technology Standards

While jumping right into the technology as a strategy for relationship management may seem odd, this element is incredibly important to being able to accelerate and streamline onboarding, training, and trust in a community of users. Creating technology standards helps the organization by:

- Reducing confusion for both the users and the consumers of the information, providing an "approved pathway"
- Better positioning the organization for comprehensive analytics training for all users
- Increasing adoption by offering comprehensive training tools, support, shared skills, knowledge, and potentially "no-cost" analytics if enterprise-wide agreements are funded from the top
- Achieving greater satisfaction with the services of IT, support, and accelerating the delivery projects
- Enabling agility through speed to value via enterprise licenses, shared services environments, captive development teams, and other strategies
- Reducing licensing costs for the entire organization and providing better leverage with technology vendors for discounts and lower TCO

Overall, having the broad organization work together with a common platform and process can accelerate innovative levels of the use of technology more strategically, embedding it in processes, adding more user features, and achieving better use of analytics within the organization. Having a shared understanding, knowledge, and way of working will increase collaboration and allow users to share best practices. This does not necessarily mean establishing a single "one-size-fits-all" tool or vendor, but establishing standards for the various capabilities that are used. As the technology standards take hold within the organization, projects become more manageable, best-practices guides can be established, and there are fewer "emergencies" and less "rework" for everyone.

Manage the Business Analytics Product Standards

With the establishment of standards in technology, an organization can also establish a single point of contact for responding to user queries about the Business Analytics standards for support and training, which is an essential element to the success of the program. A single point of contact for support will allow easy access to users to streamline the resolution of technical issues, reinforce user adoption, and clarify vendor relationships. The product management contact should be someone with a technical bent, but also a person who will work closely with the business to ensure requirements are met. In addition, the management of the product standards should include the task of user training, so that user adoption is not hampered by a lack of basic knowledge on the product.

Onboard and Enable the Larger Team

A common tension found in some programs is the need to get people onboard and productive quickly. If the time to onboard to a standard is not different from the time to purchase and implement a new technology, why would teams wait? There's a balance that needs to be established, but the number one priority should be getting up and running with a minimum of effort.

Here are some techniques that have proven to alleviate the barriers to user adoptions:

- **Free or low-cost access and entry:** Provide "free" access, at least on a trial basis. If users perceive that the software is both available and free—or very low-cost—the team can gain significant buy-in. The best strategy is to have a centralized funding model that will cover the software as overhead in an existing infrastructure regionally deployed. This approach will increase adoption and establish alignment to the standard. From the business users' perspective, this eliminates an immediate barrier of needing budget and resources to implement the software, and they can get up and running more quickly at a lower cost of entry.
- **Self-service:** Find the right balance of self-service and IT or analytic support. We've found that a self-service tool often can mean fewer headaches and less time-consuming support for the Business Analytics team. If users don't

have to wait for the BA team to create cubes or build reports for them, they can begin using the tool to achieve what they needed and fall into alignment with the standards sooner. Self-service is achieved by the right selection of tools that fit the needs of the user complemented by strong training and a cultural environment that allows and encourages access to information and tools. Governance is also importance in this space, as information anarchy can propagate with BA tools as easily as it has in the past with spreadsheet and other desktop tools.

- **Enterprise architecture:** With an easily expandable platform offering, ramp-up time is reduced; procurement discussions are mostly about capacity planning; support services are leveraged; consistent release management is offered; and services are more easily managed, upgraded, and aligned with other IT component strategies (e.g., database upgrades). This also enables an excellent view of the BA ecosystem and enterprise metrics on performance, and usage, as well as well-defined proven practices and governance models with clear technology roadmaps.

Establish Timely, Trusted Information

If users can't understand the data, they will not trust it. If they don't trust it, they'll stop using it. If it is slow to be delivered, they won't wait for it. Confidence in the Business Analytics Program requires confidence that the information is easily understood, accurate, and timely.

To reach those results, a strong collaboration between IT and the business units is a prerequisite, and the relationship should be a dynamic one in which there is a free flow of suggestions for improvement from both sides. The program isn't the single domain of any individual department, but an organizational resource designed for the benefit of all parties.

Create a Culture and Encourage Collaboration

To build a Business Analytics Program and projects that the organization needs and users want, the Business Analytics Program needs to be a partnership between the various stakeholders to form individual project strategies, determine information requirements, and work out issues. Maintaining momentum, celebrating success, and communicating openly are extremely important. Delivering the message from the top-down and through the organization will encourage modeling of the behavior. Managing by analytics needs to be a part of every management team culture and must be driven through the team by management.

It is also important to establish a culture of learning from mistakes. Often, stakeholders will be reticent to place measurable goals on initiatives with which they have no former experience. They may be in fear of being accountable for areas that couldn't previously be measured with ease. From the top down, an analytic culture that drives usage to improve—rather than penalize—the business will create a culture that is free of fear and more willing to collaborate and participate.

Developing champions in every area of the business that can help celebrate success-es, communicate benefits, and share best practices or train new users will create the momentum throughout the organization. This point is important as well at the executive level—to ensure executive teams are bought into and champion the efforts within their own teams. Developing specialized training for executive members may be necessary to ensure they are able to understand the value and engage in the program to help champion the effort.

A culture of leading, rather than managing people to follow strict processes and rules, is also a way to secure buy-in. Empowering users, asking for their advice, and engaging them throughout the process will increase collaboration and drive new, innova-tive ideas into the program. It can be tempting— and sometimes necessary—to drive strict processes and rules to encourage teams to follow standards and guidelines, but a balance of creating empowerment and compliance is necessary to increase success.

> "Establishing strong collaboration with users may mean that you'll need to bend or break some of the longstanding rules in IT. Rather than waiting to fulfill requests through a Demand Management process, you'll need to be more proactive with users to help them understand where new opportunities may lie."
>
> —*Brian Green*

Build the Communication Strategy

To execute on driving an analytic culture, it is important to communicate the value of the Business Analytics Program throughout the organization.

Organizations that clearly understand the benefits of the program will enlist a broader user base and a stronger, more visible support of the program's endeavors. This requires information sharing and a strong communications strategy.

> "I've found that often just providing a playground or a sandbox will be enough of a breeding ground for the curious, tech-savvy, early adopters to create new proofs of concept."
>
> —*John Boyer*

Here are some important techniques for bolstering the communication strategy:

- Quantify and communicate the potential benefits that the program or project can deliver—for example, hours saved, costs reduced, or efficiency gained.
- Develop a visioning exercise, proof-of-concept, or technology showcase for the Business Analytics Program.

- Enlist vendors to demonstrate the software and techniques that support the profile. Tie your proof-of-concept directly to the strategic goals of your organization.
- Provide opportunities for real users to showcase how they are using the Business Analytics technology in their businesses or areas.

When deploying something as large-scale as Business Analytics, project champions and their teams should be prepared to *showcase the successes* and use a wide variety of communication tactics to acquire the mandate and then get users progressively more involved throughout the execution phase.

KEY CONCEPT

Demonstrating the value proposition of your Business Analytics initiative through a marquee project and building on that success with other wins, communications tactics, demos, training, and recognition will help maintain high-level interest in Business Analytics and keep the whole company interested, engaged, and involved.

While gaining widespread buy-in and executive support for your Business Analytics initiative is absolutely key, the support has to be sustained once it has been achieved. Early buy-in must also snowball into broad user adoption during execution. The best way to keep the momentum going and get the troops on board is to showcase your Business Analytics initiative—communicate success and demonstrate value, and keep on doing it.

Start telling the story through email campaigns, word of mouth, face-to-face meetings, and other means. Your marquee project will demonstrate that the value of Business Analytics far outweighs the change it requires. As new projects begin to reap benefits, regularly send out an email newsletter with user tips, success stories, news, and recognition. Use your intranet to provide Business Analytics FAQs, tips, a user blog, news, and other information. Hold regular lunch-and-learn sessions showcasing successes, tips and tricks, or business usability and adaptability. Implement telephone, webcast, and face-to-face meetings where benefits and projects can be evangelized regularly.

It is key to remember that the initiative is always about the people who need to be engaged and involved and about the shared expertise that can generate innovation and opportunities. This means that the Center of Excellence has to generate excitement, engagement, and buy-in with the team regularly throughout the life of the program.

Think of your people and the people involved in the Business Analytics Program as your strongest viral evangelists and communicators. They will spread word of the program's success, but you want to maintain a communications strategy that supports their efforts. So prepare for a continual communication campaign that has room to grow and expand in concert with the successes of each subsequent analytics project. Create a formalized plan that includes scheduled quarterly face-to-face meetings or regular conferences with key stakeholders, and include program initiatives in regular internal communications as well as viral, email, social media, or print strategies.

Train Your Users

Establishing a training program is an essential step to wider user adoption and the growth of an analytic culture. Some users may not adopt the culture if they cannot use the tools with ease. Others might be uncomfortable. Many may be embarrassed if they do not feel competent in their analytic skills. Hold a set of formal and informal training programs, and use a combination of in-class and online training courses to meet the preferences and needs of the business users, but understand that training both on technical competency and organizational data is a requirement to gain adoption.

People: Success or Derailment

The Program Office needs to ensure there is continual focus on the "People" aspect of the Business Analytics Program. People will contribute to the success or potentially derail a Business Analytics Program—not necessarily because they are aiming to see its defeat, but most often because of a lack of understanding of the goals, the value, or what the team is trying to achieve. With clear communication, training, and a collaborative approach to Business Analytics, the program team can create momentum, discover champions and partners, and scale the program broadly throughout the organization—contributing to the overall success of the business. People will need to not only understand the larger goals of the program to feel connected but also develop trust and confidence in the team and its processes. Keeping a team engaged will also be a balancing act between delivering processes that will create efficiencies and keep the program agile vs. processes that frustrate and demotivate users.

A best practice is to create an Analytics Center of Excellence that may comprise a number of structured or virtual teams with clear roles and responsibilities that supports the overall program. This Center of Excellence will change and grow over time, but at the root of it is the goal to develop innovation, empowerment, analytic skill, and program success. Organizations that establish such a center typically outperform in every area measured, according to a Business Applications Research Center[2] study. These Centers of Excellence achieve more buy-in, consistency, and therefore more budget and momentum than silo approaches in an organization.

In the next section, we look at a case study where a successful implementation of a Center of Excellence achieved quantifiable outcomes. We then take a focused look at various organizational designs for the Analytics Center of Excellence and provide a checklist of items that need to be considered when managing the "People" element of the Business Analytics Program. In the next chapter, we discuss the closely linked "Process" part of the equation—a part that will either contribute to how inspired the team can remain or cause them to abandon the project.

---

[2] "Organization of Business Intelligence." Business Applications Research Center, Wurtzberg, August 2010.

Case Study on People: Martin's Point Health Care

From guest authors Jeff Guevin, Manager of BI Architecture,
and Eric Place, Manager of BI Reporting & Analysis,
Martin's Point Health Care

Establishing a Business Intelligence Competency Center drives excellence in analytics and decision making

> "Analytics, report creation, and understanding data content have a long learning curve. Being surrounded by experts in a BICC greatly shortens that learning curve. The ability to ask questions as well as being mentored by others allows us to onboard analysts faster and with greater success."
>
> *—Eric Place, Manager of BI Reporting and Analysis,*
> *Martin's Point Health Care*

Martin's Point Health Care Overview

Martin's Point Health Care is a not-for-profit health care delivery organization founded in 1981 in Portland, Maine. Its mission is twofold:

1. Provide primary health care through group practices and health care centers
2. Administer TRICARE Prime, Medicare Advantage, and commercial health plans

Today, Martin's Point serves approximately 129,000 clinic patients and health plan members in Maine, New Hampshire, northern New York, and Pennsylvania.

Martin's Point Health Care had a goal to improve both its delivery of care and health plan management. To accomplish this goal, Martin's Point felt it necessary to focus more intently on gaining visibility into information that would assist with decision making across all areas of the organization. Key questions needed to be more quickly answered to empower management to make better decisions for both patients and health administrators.

Martin's Point Health Care felt that it needed to understand its complex systems landscape to support faster access to more accurate information and provide management with greater insight into the organization's key metrics. The goal was to help clinical managers monitor patients' treatments and outcomes more effectively by strategically shifting the way reporting was delivered to the organization.

Martin's Point determined that with a strategy that aligned to top goals, and to effectively implement an analytics system that would drive results, creating a Business Intelligence Competency Center (BICC) was the logical, most cost-effective means to achieve its strategic goals.

Driving Improvements with a Culture and People Focus

The overall organizational structure—as with most organizations—was designed with silos of people, information, and goals that, while highly effective in maintaining focus on the business areas, did not always lend themselves to collaboratively using information to improve results enterprise-wide. In addition, Martin's Point operates in both the health care delivery and health plan sectors. These vastly different business areas have very different reporting and analysis needs and require a complex landscape of IT systems, which includes seven enterprise applications and 20 separate databases across 13 different business units. Prior to the implementation of the BICC, the diversity of systems coupled with no centralized data repository made it difficult for Martin's Point to collect, consolidate, and disseminate information. Consequently, reporting had become an overly complex process, requiring multiple queries into numerous systems with subsequent manual aggregation of results.

With a goal to improve decision making, the organization realized it would have to provide faster access to the most up-to-date information. This level of insight would help clinical managers track process and outcome measures for patients and would allow the health plan greater understanding of its operations.

The complexity and variety of its IT systems made the organization realize that it was not simply a matter of finding the right software tools, but that a strategic shift in the way the company was organized around information was required. Martin's Point also realized that the way analytics was perceived within the organization needed to shift away from silo-driven reporting to a more holistic, efficient, enterprise-wide approach.

To facilitate the goals of faster, more accurate reporting, Martin's Point Health Care embarked on a new Business Analytics Strategy. Core to this strategy was a focus on how to align people, skills, and culture to deliver on the strategy and value it could provide. These values guided the evolution of the Martin's Point Business Intelligence Competency Center.

The new BICC allowed a focused team to cross information silos and understand the strategic value of data, as well as create processes that would reduce the time required to collect data and generate reports from an average of two weeks to near *real-time* reporting. The BICC was then able to influence a culture of performance, collaboration, and trust that allowed the organization to fully leverage its data.

The BICC now helps to deliver hundreds of successful projects each year that assist end users in gaining greater insight into operations, as well as monitor and improve key performance metrics. Some leading examples of its success include:

- **Health plan management:** A wide range of reports aid health plan managers in understanding and improving per-member per-month costs and other key metrics. For example, an "outlier report" plots the variance of cost and utilization metrics by physician specialty to identify areas for further research to improve performance. This reporting process draws attention to problem areas and helps to identify root causes, leading to more efficient and cost-effective health plan management.

- **Clinical practice:** Specific reports help clinicians identify gaps in care and ensure that each patient receives the treatments he or she needs. For example, patients with chronic conditions such as diabetes or congestive heart failure require regular tests to monitor their conditions. The BICC developed reports that identify any patient whose tests are due, ensuring that clinicians contact the patient to arrange an appointment. By mining the electronic medical records, the patient's test results can also be analyzed to identify areas for intervention to improve patient outcomes.

- **Error monitoring of end users:** Administrators within the BICC have developed a capability to report on the *quality* of its own end users' reporting processes. For example, if a user is struggling to get a specific report to work properly, the reporting system automatically emails the BI administrators about the problem. An administrator can then intervene to fix the problem directly or, alternatively, give the user additional training so that in the future the user is better able to serve himself or herself. This proactive approach helps to promote the adoption of analytics within the company because users receive the support they need without even having to ask.

Best Practices in People

Martin's Point Health Care's BICC has developed a set of best practices that greatly streamlines and enhances the overall implementation of Business Analytics. These practices communicate the value of the BICC to management while simultaneously empowering users to work more quickly and more effectively in their jobs. These best practices include:

- ✓ **Executive support and creation of a culture of performance:** By gaining executive buy-in and trust in the program, a culture of performance has been driven top-down and through the various units of the organization with the help of the BICC.

- ✓ **Concentrating BI skills and knowledge:** By utilizing a centralized BICC, Martin's Point has been able to define and spread its BI/Analytics best practices across the company. The BICC drives the culture of analytics and provides the skills and training necessary. The business users now speak the same language as the BICC, which helps department-based analysts find solutions and address business needs more quickly and efficiently. With specialist teams created within the BICC, users know who to contact for guidance and assistance. For instance, architecture, administration, and reporting teams each focus on specific aspects of BI competency but retain the flexibility to support each other when required.

✓ **Structured training:** The BICC at Martin's Point has established structured training programs to help business users *self-serve* their reporting needs. The training ensures that BI tools and data are used correctly by non-BICC analysts— delivering accurate, actionable, and consistent information to all business units. Training ensures that business users don't have to wait in line for their projects to be handled by a BICC reporting analyst but instead can use the structured training, plus their own skills and knowledge, to gain faster access to information.

Proven Business Benefits

> "Our senior management really bought into the BICC, and we have earned respect across the business by delivering successful projects over time. There has been a culture shift in the way analytics is used, and the BICC is seen as consultants who serve the needs of the business, rather than just guys who write reports."
>
> *—Jeff Guevin, Manager of BI Architecture, Martin's Point Health Care*

The success of Martin's Point Health Care's BICC has been impressive. In a brief period of time, the organization has:

- Enabled the BICC to act as a consultant to their customers, providing user training and spreading best practices instead of being perceived merely as a reporting resource.
- Substantially reduced the time it takes to collect data and perform analyses. Reports that used to take two weeks to assemble can now be generated in seconds with a few mouse clicks.
- Eased the learning curve for new BICC team members by surrounding them with expert help.
- Empowered end users to perform analyses themselves, reducing report-building workload for the BICC team.
- Provided rapid, accurate insight into key financial performance metrics, such as per-member per-month costs, helping health plan managers monitor medical expense.
- Helped clinicians improve patient outcomes—for example, identifying patients who need to come in for tests and monitoring the results of those tests to help manage chronic conditions.

How have these benefits been demonstrated to the organization?

A Nucleus Research ROI study[3] reveals that the creation of the Martin's Point BICC has resulted in tangible ROI results of 1,185 percent per year, leading to full return within just one month and total benefits of more than $1 million (Table 4).

Return on Investment Summary	
Annual ROI:	1,185%
Payback period:	1 month
Average annual benefit:	$335,250
Total Three-Year Benefits	
Direct:	$540,000
Indirect:	$465,750
Total:	$1,005,750
Pie chart: Direct = 54% / Indirect = 46%	
Source: *ROI Case Study: IBM Cognos BI Competency Center, Martin's Point Health Care (Document J40). Nucleus Research. Boston, MA: June 2009.*	

Table 4: ROI Results for Martin's Point Health Care's BICC

Martin's Point Health Care has grown rapidly from 300 employees in 2009 to over 800 today. There has also been rapid growth in the adoption of Business Intelligence. Demand for reporting has grown tenfold over the same period, as more business areas have embraced the power of analytics.

Business users can now generate the reports they need without support from the BICC team. The user-friendliness of the Business Analytics solution, combined with the BICC's concerted efforts to provide comprehensive training and spread best practices, have increased the organization's analytic capability.

Martin's Point continues to evolve its BICC with the growth of the organization and considers it to be a strategic center as well as a competitive advantage for the organization.

---

[3] *ROI Case Study: IBM Cognos BI Competency Center, Martin's Point Health Care (Document J40).* Nucleus Research. Boston, MA: June 2009.

Practical Tips for Organizing People: Designing an Analytics Center of Excellence

Organizational design can accelerate or hinder a Business Analytics Program. Whereas we speak about the *Business Analytics Program* and its elements in this book, we refer to the specific organizational design concept that supports the program as the *Analytics Center of Excellence.*

As we mentioned in the main chapter for the "People" element, early-stage programs tend to be smaller and more virtual in nature. Such a program may consist of a few cross-functional team members who collaborate and innovate together on a regular basis. It may be spearheaded by a manager or business owner coupled with IT and analytic experts. Figure 19 depicts a typical early-stage program.

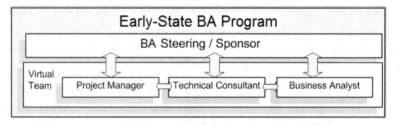

Figure 19: Early-Stage BA Program

As the program matures, it will likely grow larger, with more formal fixed team members—located either in IT or in the line of business where the program originated (Figure 20).

As the program gains momentum and more business areas get involved, the organizational design may adjust again—becoming either highly centralized or dispersed among the business areas (Figure 21).

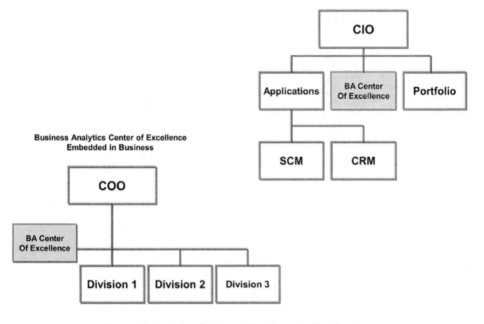

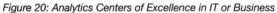

Figure 20: Analytics Centers of Excellence in IT or Business

Figure 21: Virtual Teams by Function

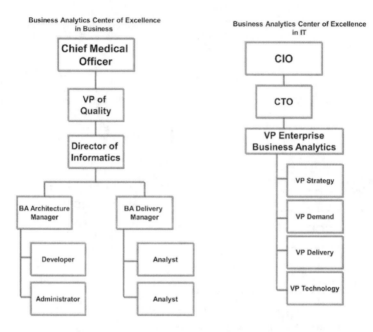

Figure 22: Growing Centers of Excellence Organizational Charts

It may also become more virtual in nature, with large centers (Figure 22).

As user adoption grows, the Analytics Center of Excellence will need to accommodate more teams of users; in Figure 23, you can see an example of a core team that is built to interface across a wide user population, with Centers of Excellence team members defined with roles and responsibilities in the business. This configuration requires a larger central program team that would manage the community, communication, evangelism, and program management tasks.

We believe that an emerging future state would include a Chief Analytics Officer who would manage the overall program, with a centralized program team that manages a strongly connected program across many cross-functional teams within the organization. Figure 24 depicts this organizational design. This approach enables an executive to balance priorities and demands across a diverse set of users and ensure that cadence, communication, and collaboration are at the heart of it—setting the agenda for strategy refresh and execution and gaining the highest value and cost of ownership.

Again, how your Analytics Center of Excellence is designed will be completely up to the organizational culture that exists as well as the maturity level, but we hope that by sharing these various organizational structures, we can help provide ideas and assist you in choosing the optimal design for your organization.

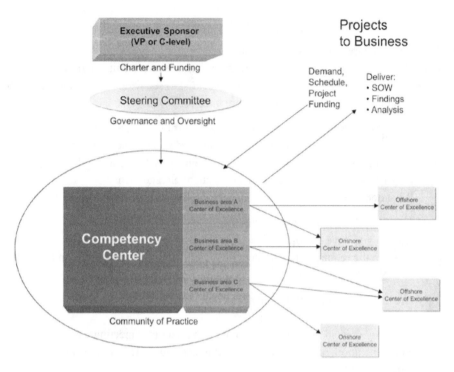

Figure 23: Maturing Center of Excellence

Figure 24: Future State Center of Excellence

People Checklist

In the "People" chapter, we discussed a number of program areas that should be considered for your Business Analytics Program to implement a suitable organizational design and drive an analytic culture. Use this checklist to see which areas might be useful to integrate and manage over time in your organization:

✓ Have you assessed your current analytic maturity and analytic culture?

✓ Do you have executive involvement, and have you mapped your stakeholders?

✓ How can you drive more executive involvement? Choose a couple of executives who are not yet involved and create a plan to engage them.

✓ What does your organizational design look like today, and is it suitable?

  ◦ Are roles and responsibilities clear?

  ◦ Do you have the right talent in your organization?

  ◦ Are the required stakeholders involved—mixing business, IT, and analytic talent?

✓ Are there communication vehicles in place that you are using to build momentum?

✓ Have you created a communication plan that includes meetings, email communication, and inclusion in existing communication vehicles in your organization?

✓ Do you have a training program in place?

Chapter 4
Key #4: Process

In the last chapter, we discussed how organizational design and managing the culture of analytics can create success in the Business Analytics Program. We have already started to discuss many of the processes that need to be put in place because people and process are closely tied. Processes that are clear and understood will help people work together more efficiently. However, a successful Business Analytics Program requires processes to be established that maintain a balance between agility and structure. On the one hand, we must ensure that agility is retained to address the rapidly changing needs of the business. On the other hand, we must also ensure the right processes are applied that will increase efficiencies and maintain effective governance of the program.

To achieve that balance, strong collaboration between technology departments and business units is required, addressing the challenges of data and information silos, disparate processes, and technology maturity. In many ways, building such a program is similar to piecing together a massive jigsaw puzzle of information resources (people, processes, data, and infrastructure). Each organization is unique, and each element of the construction is different. Each population of users has individual nuances, as well as cultural and political ecosystems, that filter the way the users view the world around them. Consequently, the processes that you need will continually require creativity, flexibility, customization, and adaptation. Much of the exercise is around the complexity of change management of people and processes as well as technology.

Defining Our Terms	
Effectiveness	The ability to address the needs of the organization and its stakeholders.
Agility	The ability to change directions, if necessary, and address the needs *in a timely way*.

Although there is no "one-size-fits-all" approach that will work for every organization, several examples of efficient proven practices in process implementation can be viewed to construct the right set of processes required for *your* organization. What is important in implementing processes is to keep an eye on what is right to be implemented based on the timing and maturity of the program. We need to ensure that the stakeholders review the processes end-to-end to determine how to maintain agility and efficiency—and review them over time to ensure they still make sense as the program evolves.

What follows is a look at a number of critical processes that we feel are essentials to an agile analytics program. These processes can help the Business Analytics Program to remain both effective and agile in meeting the needs of your organization. In this chapter, we discuss:

- Processes to achieve Business Analytics Program agility and maturity
- Identifying stakeholders and kicking off the project
- Documenting processes for communication, education, and adoption
- Proven practice sharing
- Creating an advise and consult framework
- Development processes
- Requirements gathering
- Governance
- Defining processes for technology standards, support, and innovation
- Maintaining a culture of process agility

Maturity of the Business Analytics Program

If we look at the Analytics Quotient Maturity Model as an example by which we can apply process, a typical pattern of the early stages is that very few processes are put in place. This lack of processes results in a chaotic information environment; because each organization operates in a silo and works on its own analytic initiative, very few processes might exist, and they will exist differently within each silo. Indeed, they may be effective in those silos, but as a company you may not be efficient. Even something as basic as who to go to for assistance may be confusing to business users looking for the information they need for business insight.

> "It's always hard to find the balance between no process and too much process."
>
> —*John Boyer*

As the program matures and develops, the requirement for processes becomes clearer—a way to establish some basic rules, frameworks, and ways to manage the inundation of requests. This need can result in the over-engineering of processes as the organization matures, increasing the length of time it takes to achieve the level of insight required by the business. Gates and roadblocks among the multiple stakeholders involved in getting a project off the ground can become a waiting game that derails the programs and leaves teams seeking their own means and methods to get the work done.

Program leaders need to continually review the Business Analytics Program at a macro level—from different stakeholder viewpoints—reviewing the end-to-end processes that have been put in place to manage the various requirements. The key to running a successful initiative and determining where either value is achieved or program derailment can occur is this continual review and evolution of the program.

Stakeholder Identification and New Project Start

One of the most basic processes that needs to be put in place in early maturity levels is one that provides accessibility to the team and a clear understanding of how employees throughout an organization can get involved in the program. What is the program about? Who can they turn to? Are there experts in their own business area to whom they can reach out? What has the program done to date? How can individuals, groups, or teams get involved? What processes, practices, architectures, and technology standards need to be considered?

This process requires a well-managed knowledge-sharing repository—most often a website, team room, or collaboration area that is easy to find within the organization (e.g., on the enterprise, business domain, or IT portal). This repository welcomes the teams into the area where documents are kept, best practices are shared, and roles, responsibilities, and processes are outlined for the team. Having a knowledge-sharing repository that can capture all contact details, news, information, and onboarding requirements will help to more easily onboard team members.  **KEY CONCEPT**

As we spoke about earlier in the development and evolution of the organizational design, the subject matter experts and key points of contact should be clearly identified to encourage collaboration and engagement among team members. By clearly defining, with open communication to new members of the team, who they can contact and how a new project or analytics initiative can get off the ground, the risk of new project silos can be decreased.

Onboarding and Enablement

To welcome more team members into the program, ease of onboarding and enablement within the program are critical. How does the group access the tools and integrate their data, and whom do they go to for training? Having clear processes and training programs in place that ease the onboarding process can begin a strong relationship with a new team member who may have been hesitant to make a change. Managing change is always difficult, and first impressions definitely count. When designing your program, communications, and information available on the knowledge repository, you'll want to make sure that you have basic questions covered:

- Who are the key contacts for the program, and for what are they responsible?
- What is the process to get engaged, and what steps are involved?
- Where can team members go to learn about the tools available or get training on the tools?
- Who can they go to for expertise on how to design metrics?
- Who do they go to with suggestions?
- How do they keep on top of news, communications, or other updates that may occur over time?

Easing the onboarding process will go a long way to bringing new champions on board and gaining trust in your users. Ensure specifically that this process is kept light and efficient—if it is too difficult to join up front, team members may abandon quickly.

Communication, Education, and Adoption

There is no question in our minds that communication and education on the Business Analytics tools and processes ultimately will enhance and increase user adoption. But too often a communication strategy is not introduced into a program as a discrete element that needs time and resources, and educational efforts become fragmented in the silos of the enterprise itself. Increased user adoption will result from communication of the value that is being delivered, clear shared goals that everyone strives to achieve, and inclusion and collaboration among teams with strong educational and training efforts at the core.

> "Maintaining these resources, and documenting lessons learned, allows the organization to get smarter with each new project. As philosopher George Santayana once said, 'Those who cannot remember the past are condemned to repeat it.'"
>
> —*John Boyer*

In terms of communication, efforts to showcase, market, and hold stakeholder meetings—at executive, management, and working team levels—requires resource time, efforts, and clear strategies and processes to ensure communication happens. The creation of emails, newsletters, value maps, roadmaps, websites, collaboration technologies, and best practices requires time, effort, and budget consideration. The benefit? Less politics and increased collaboration across teams that reduce time, costs, and the risk of project failures over the long run.

In addition, Business Analytics educational offerings need to be continually monitored for their effectiveness, with elements examined individually for value. Wherever possible, the elements of the education offerings should be converged into a program with hands-on experience with the tools and access to expert users. This kind of educational program can significantly increase users' productivity and empower them to develop a vibrant analytics community. Moreover, we feel that those users who have mastered the tools should be recognized and nurtured as expert resources, to be utilized for the benefit of the Business Analytics Program as a whole.

The educational offerings provided by the program can also build upon the communities of users by providing a forum for communicating successes. We found great value in providing special training seminars for broadcasting highly successful analytics techniques. Education can span from technical training, to the actions of communicating news of analytics updates, to notifying users about changes within the analytics organization and instituting best practices resources to streamline learning.

> "Communicating the what, why, and how of your Business Analytics Program and providing a forum to showcase success stories on a regular basis are key to increasing user adoption and to maintaining momentum in your Business Analytics Program."
>
> —*Kay Van De Vanter*

A successful, agile education and communication initiative will:

- Coordinate educational processes that increase user adoption
- Measure and monitor training outcomes and adoption levels
- Reduce the overlap of training services between departments and silos
- Identify both *power users* and *problem users,* and customize outreach accordingly
- Enable change to be enjoyed and not feared
- Focus on overall educational quality
- Increase collaboration across sites and silos to increase productivity and the value of the Business Analytics Program
- Promote and market the Business Analytics Program and its benefits

> **Note**
> Read the above list again and think how you can turn each of these measures of success into actual metrics within your organization.

Proven Practice Sharing

One of the most powerful techniques for enhancing the agility of the Business Analytics Program is the sharing of information called Proven Practices.

Proven Practices are generally accepted, standardized techniques, methods, or processes that have proven themselves over time to accomplish given tasks. Proven Practices are practical guidelines gleaned from professional experiences in Business Analytics. They can be from internal sources or external sources (e.g., this book).

The concept of a Proven Practices discipline is that, with proper steps, checks, and testing, desired outcomes can be delivered more effectively or efficiently with fewer problems and unforeseen complications.

Some organizations start by building a Business Analytics Proven Practices regimen with rigorous testing, management input, and detailed documentation, toward the goal of developing Proven Practices that can be broadly implemented across multiple sectors within the organization. Other organizations treat their Proven Practices in a more agile manner—as organic, evolving guidelines, templates, or checklists that can accelerate implementation, user adoption, and organizational efficiencies.

No matter how Proven Practices are implemented, the key is to *share* and *promote* them throughout the organization, in a timely manner, using central websites, shared media, educational seminars, newsletters, or any other means of internal organizational publication.

By documenting Proven Practices, the organization builds the repository of useful guidelines that can help others avoid pitfalls in implementation, speed deployments, and provide better support to the Business Analytics community. It's cost effective because it *shortcuts* the learning process that every new project initiates. It increases user adoption levels because it promotes the success of the analytics program, encourages emulation, and offers a measure of proof to reluctant entities within the organization, demonstrating that the analytics process can work for them.

Proven Practice sharing:

- Identifies what works
- Communicates success to users and management
- Establishes user/management feedback loops
- Builds and expands collaboration and community across silos/departments
- Strengthens user adoption
- Reinforces standards
- Ultimately, increases efficiencies and reduces costs

Developing an Advise and Consult Framework

> "I've seen that outside consultants often are the ones to share information between departments within an organization. We can learn from that and create that same culture, where a central group of internal consultants share information within the organization."
>
> *—John Boyer*

One process we've found to sustain and expand the analytic community is opening up the analytics team with a framework of advising and consulting to other areas of the enterprise. This framework can develop a Business Analytics knowledge center—which can develop into the Center of Excellence—where centralized analytics resources, tools, and methodologies can be made available to others as informal or formalized consulting services that empower the broader community. The set of skills and knowledge that the organization has developed then becomes a much broader and more powerful resource for the entire enterprise. In addition to being a resource team to lend expertise, the team's goal is to empower groups, users, and the overall community to self-serve and become competent in the tools, data, and processes.

From an organizational perspective, an analytics framework for advising and consulting:

- Enables convergence of skills and knowledge through competency centers
- Reduces overlap of analytics services
- Increases the agility of the organization to respond to new requirements
- Reinforces the credo of a "consistent version of truth" that empowers management
- Emphasizes Business Analytics methodologies and successes
- Spreads the culture of Business Analytics throughout the organization
- Leads to greater user adoption

The ability of the Business Analytics team to reach out to other business units, across boundaries of embedded silos and diverse departments, increases the strategic value of the analytics program. As the Business Analytics Program grows throughout the organization, it empowers users to achieve new efficiencies with new tools for the advancement of management's goals.

Streamlining Requirements Gathering

A first step in kicking off an analytic endeavor—requirements gathering—may be one of the hardest tasks, to ensure enough information is captured without confusing a business user or team with complex terms, questions, and technical specifications. Many organizations refine and evolve their requirements planning processes into a myriad of IT request forms, project scope interviews, scheduling steps, and review processes—all before any action is approved or budgeted. While these numerous steps may be appropriate in some organizations and for some applications, they can significantly delay an analytics program. Why?

Consider the number of potential sources of information an analytics program may need to tap to deliver its promises to management. Think about how complex and detailed those steps may become if multiple departments, silos, business units, or subsidiaries are included. Imagine the redundancy of the requirements planning and the timelines to productivity if all these gathering processes are followed across all responsible entities in a large corporation. The scope of the requirements cycle itself can be immense, and the outcome can become detrimental to adoption of the analytics process.

Therefore, we believe that the processes for requirements gathering for Business Analytics need to be examined and streamlined wherever possible. The difference between requirements gathering and creating an IT spec document needs to be considered. The process should, in our opinion, be reduced to the minimum number of steps that meet the needs of the particular silo/department/business unit to get the process of actual information delivery up and running as quickly and as efficiently as possible.

This streamlining should include:

- Creating the document based on the fundamental questions and business processes—not jumping into solutioning and design
- Coordinating cross-platform/cross-departmental requirements to reduce the number of steps and forms required to spec the analytics process
- Improving communication between business users and developers
- Identifying and implementing the minimal set of requirements planning steps that more quickly allow the design and build phases to begin
- Accepting the fact that requirements documentation may not be completed until the end of the development cycle
- Keeping stakeholders informed of the evolving requirements
- Reinforcing and leveraging standard tools, proven practices, and agile processes
- Moving to an iterative cycle of plan–deliver–deploy–repeat that is much different from traditional IT projects, which tend to use a waterfall approach

There is no question that the discipline of requirements gathering is the quintessential tool for delivering positive analytics outcomes. But the processes themselves can be customized and consolidated to deliver better requirements that are more agile and responsive to the needs of the organization as a whole.

KEY CONCEPT

> "Many people jump to 'solutioning' too quickly, rather than starting with the business questions and outcomes they are looking to achieve. Start with the questions and have a collaborative process—you might get more than you expect if you ask a business question rather request a tool."
>
> —*Brian Green*

Agility in Development

While a strict discipline in "Agile Development" has been developed, this is not what we are referring to in this section of the book. We believe that in order to achieve agility in Business Analytics development, what is required is better collaboration throughout the entire Business Analytics development cycle. It is communication, rather than a 12-page requirements document. In the past, Business Analytics has often tried to use a deployment model that follows traditional development cycles—gathering requirements, developing a finished product, and presenting it back to the requester. The result has often been the inability to actually translate the user requirements into the expected result—which means iteration is required. An example of this might be agile pairing, where a report developer sits with a trained business user and a business analyst to create a report and capture the requirements at the same time. Some of the benefits include knowledge sharing, evolving business requirements, and a report that meets the needs of the business.

We believe that the methodology by which Business Analytics projects need to be handled is a more collaborative, iterative one—requiring constant collaboration as the project rolls out. Of course, requirements gathering is a basic step in the process, but requiring a long form to be filled out by a business user with little communication will certainly deter collaboration. In addition, we have observed that Business Analytics projects will show increased value with greater satisfaction when users can visualize and understand the possible options available to them and are allowed to refine their requirements through the learning process. This requires a series of iterative steps that will help to shape, guide, and refine requirements according to the expected business outcomes. Often, users don't know what they don't know—and as they learn and see the art of the possible, their requirements are refined.

> **"The goal of the agile report development process is always to get to a 'demo-able' product quickly."**
>
> *—John Boyer*

At the highest level, this methodology will require:

1. *Initial discovery and requirements gathering*—at the level of the business questions that need to be answered. At this stage, users need to refrain from trying to jump to a solution or focus on tools at the outset. While they may envision a specific dashboard and visuals that they would like to see, they may not actually understand that there are better ways to achieve their goals than what they asked for at the start. Drill to the business requirement, not the solution. This is the hard part. The Business Requirements document should be just that: business requirements. How the team can meet those requirements, technically, should come later and must be mapped to the business requirements.

2. *An estimate and timeline for project steps* to gain a shared understanding of the complexity and details behind what is required. These can help to reduce the initial scope and potentially build out a plan for stages to evolve the project to deliver immediate value and then pragmatic steps to achieve additional value over time.

3. *A rough build, or storyboard, of the analytics project*—demonstrating options, refining the data and metrics, and outlining the required best practices. This step allows the opportunity for additional input and feedback.

4. *Delivery of the initial prototype* with input for refinements and a repeat process for each additional step in the project plan and a review of the plan to ensure priorities are being captured.

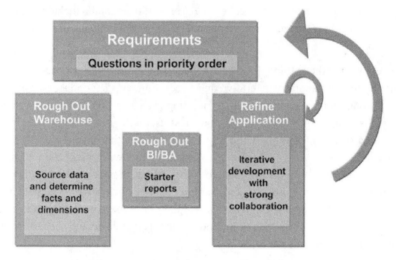

Figure 25: IBM Agile BI Development (2011)

In short, projects cannot be put on hold until they are perfect or receive the perfect requirements. The process is a constant, fluid, and collaborative one. The diagram in Figure 25, which depicts a process used at IBM, helps to demonstrate this process.

The Business Analytics Program also needs to have a transition strategy so that business requirements are not put on hold while everyone waits for data to be acquired, cleaned, transformed, and made available in the data warehouse. A process should be put in place that not only allows iterative Business Analytics development but provides an interim means to allow access to data so that projects do not go underground and create their own data sources that do not align to the Business Analytics Strategy.

Governance

As the Business Analytics program matures, analytics governance becomes increasingly important to the organization. Governance enables the organization to identify, validate, and protect a consistent version of information that is so essential for accurate reports.

The discipline of analytics governance should naturally address the convergence of processes to deal with data quality, data management, data policies, business process management, and risk management. Consequently, it should also extend to the area of application and platform standards. We believe that through realistic governance processes, organizations can instill agility while maintaining positive control over the processes and methods that extract and transform data into insightful and actionable information.

Many organizations may already have governance processes, councils, or teams in place. They may already have established processes and guidelines. The Center of Excellence needs to understand how to fit into these processes and collaborate with these team members. If no governance elements exists, the business analytics program may be a great driver to get more formalized approaches started.

In our view, governance doesn't extend only to data quality and standards issues. It should also provide an evolutionary process for a company, altering a company's bureaucratic way of thinking when it sets up processes. How?

Governance processes need to be consistently reviewed, to ascertain whether they're doing the job that the organization needs to manage the program without impinging on the ability of the enterprise to meet its goals.

For instance, we've seen how agile analytics governance can uncover the needs of users, streamline processes, and accelerate the adoption of information technology across separate business units to create a consistent information reservoir that becomes the basis of reporting and decision making. Agile analytics governance is more than setting up restrictions; it's a pathfinder for achieving productivity.

> **"A lack of governance of the data can result in bad decisions, missed opportunities, risk. Collaborating closely with the teams charged with data governance is crucial to the Business Analytics Program."**
>
> —*Tracy Harris*

Analytics governance analyzes what needs to be accomplished and then sets up a *supportable route* to implement the steps to meet the goals. By doing this in a proactive way, it not only accomplishes management goals but also keeps the analytics program on track. Governance must also evolve with the program to maintain flexibility while providing necessary control points.

It does this by identifying:

- Data management/coordination processes as they pertain to the Business Analytics Program
- Change management processes that impact the program—change and version control, technology roadmaps, training and education (people change management), strategy maps, and so on
- Information platforms that are adaptable, empowering, and driven by the Business Analytics Program's strategic objectives

How can governance processes streamline and enhance the agility of analytics? Let's look at a specific example in data management and coordination.

The Business Analytics Program will pull together a variety of data sources from the various information resources within the company. But this heterogeneity of resources opens up the possibility that the information from one source may fall out of synchronization with other data resources.

When this occurs, the analytics governance process may recognize that it needs to be closely aligned with the enterprise architecture and data warehouse initiatives to work closely with the data teams, or it might determine that a Data Steward role needs to be created. Information Management teams and Business Analytics teams need to work in concert with one another to achieve their goals as they are largely dependent on one another. The Data Steward role can be to study and understand the complete architecture of the information resources used in the Business Analytics Program and can work closely with the data teams. The Data Steward is tasked with ensuring that each assigned data element:

- Has clear and unambiguous data element definition
- Does not conflict with other data elements in the metadata registry (removes duplicates, overlap, and so on)
- Is being used consistently in various computer systems
- Has adequate documentation on appropriate usage and notes
- Documents the origin and sources of authority on each metadata element
- Ensures the ongoing quality of the information
- Reduces overlap/confusion for "accurate or consistent version of truth" in metrics

Such a role may include IT database administration *and* business analysts. But the process of identifying the need for a Data Steward is a function of governance: Its value is in enhancing the trust on the part of management that the Business Analytics Program is delivering the appropriate information.

In a similar fashion, goals for governance can be defined at all levels of the enterprise so that the overall process can aid in acceptance of the Business Analytics Program by those who will actually use it. Some governance goals should include:

- Increasing the consistency and confidence in decision making by providing trust in the data
- Improving the security of data
- Designating accountability for the quality of information
- Enabling better planning by supervisory staff
- Minimizing or eliminating rework
- Optimizing staff effectiveness
- Establishing process performance baselines to enable improvement efforts

By monitoring how the Business Analytics governance model is utilized in the organization, the agility of the organization can be enhanced through:

- Coordinating strategy
- Reducing user/management confusion about information
- Developing common goals with realistic metrics and measurable outcomes

Agile Business Analytics governance is more than simply applying standards and restrictions; it is analyzing the overall environment and making opportunities for the deployments of information that meet the strategic needs of the organization. By establishing a proactive and robust governance committee for the Business Analytics Program, questions of usability, accuracy, and consistency can be significantly reduced. At the same time, confidence in the information will increase, supporting the strategic decisions that upper management or knowledge workers must take.

Processes for Technology, Standards, and Innovation

Often, processes are implemented to declare technology standards in an effort to reduce cost and increase IT efficiencies, including efficiencies with use of time, education, and management. However, stringent standards can also result in a one-size-fits-all mentality with little room for innovation and collaboration *that can be detrimental to the program*. To ensure that agility, innovation, and efficiency goals can be achieved, processes must be designed and put in place to continually ensure that the business needs are being met, that existing technologies are evaluated as they develop and evolve, and that new capabilities and tools are evaluated not only for their applicability to the business requirement but also for their potential to disrupt the status quo and drive an increase in TCO.

Standards and License Management

The benefits of standards are clear: reduced total cost of ownership with management, administration, education, training, and reusability all contributing to a better bottom line. Increased user adoption with the ability to produce licenses and get users off to a quick start without waiting through long procurement processes can also benefit the overall program. Better consistency, control, and governance also result from the implementation of standards, and fewer arguments over the accuracy of information with developed expertise in delivering standard definitions of information can benefit the time to decisions.

In order to achieve this, the pieces of the Business Analytics puzzle must come together with a standards management process that focuses on application standards and licensing processes. The application standards will become the basis of your collaborative information platform for all of your users; a flexible licensing model will help propel user adoption of the program.

Implementing standards will reduce application costs through volume licensing agreements that lower the per-user cost, enable a more cohesive training process, and eliminate redundant services across the enterprise.

But if the standards become too fixed, inflexible, or formalized—as sometimes happens in highly centralized organizations—the management steps themselves can become a drag on user adoption levels. How? Because the more formalized the standards process becomes, the less responsive the process *appears* to the users who need to use the Business Analytics Program. Too rigid a standard, or processes around the standard, may restrict experimentation, interfere with vendor upgrades to new release levels, and discourage the organization from moving forward with technology advances—thereby increasing costs, reducing business benefit, and causing IT and business teams to seek out other solutions or revert to a silo approach.

Standards Management: A Nuanced Approach

Our approach to standards management is more nuanced than merely providing a strict standards regime. We believe the implementation of Business Analytics standards—whether by standardizing applications, formalizing processes, or assigning standardized implementation steps—needs to be carefully monitored and periodically reviewed as an ecosystem for the user community to ensure that it is not overly restrictive, inappropriately complex, or obstructive to the use of resources and technologies.

Instead of rigidly holding to standards, we believe in constantly monitoring the standards process itself. We believe the Business Analytics team can best identify procedural bottlenecks that are impinging on user adoption, identify new opportunities for technology refreshment, and simplify the processes that define and develop the Business Analytics standards. This includes many of the critical elements of Business Analytics software licensing.

For instance, many organizations pursue a policy that specifically assigns licenses to users, based on the needs defined by their departments. In these organizations, the licenses are strictly tied to departments, individuals, or computers, and the departmental budgets are appropriately charged back. This policy naturally reduces the expenses for the organization as a whole and decreases the incidence of expensive but unused license resources. However, this same policy can also restrict user adoption levels and actually slow the implementation of the Business Analytics Program as a whole. How?

If the IT standard licensing software process is too rigid, potential users in departments or business units—users that need to join the Business Analytics Program—can get bogged down with IT requests, departmental budgetary cycles, and extraneous bureaucratic steps. We believe this process should become streamlined.

What we encourage is the purchase of "extra" licenses—either individually or through volume licensing agreements—that retains a set number of unassigned licenses available for immediate assignment and use. By maintaining this arsenal of licensing resources, new users can be quickly brought into the Business Analytics Program: They escape the immediate budgetary approval practices, can begin training before departmental budgetary approval, and can populate new Business Analytics subsystems quickly. At the same time, this practice of *onboarding* new users quickly permits users to move ahead without forcing them to seek their solutions outside the approved software standards. This small change in a standards model helps build momentum for the program and still reinforces the application standards that have been implemented. It reduces time to productivity for the users and demonstrates the agility of the Business Analytics Program to quickly respond to the needs of the organization as a whole.

KEY CONCEPT

In summary, establishing application standards:

- Reduces cost
- Establishes a collaborative platform
- Enables cost-effective training
- Gives a company a seat at the vendor table for enhancement requests

At the same time, creating a flexible software license policy:

- Reduces time to business productivity
- Enables rapid user adoption
- Removes administrative obstacles to implementation
- Allows for developing cost-effective infrastructure options

In addition, a flexible approach to standards and a culture of collaboration instilled into the program can also enable continual innovation. Tasking teams with experimenting with new technologies, understanding how they can enhance or disrupt the overall initiative, and keeping lines of communication open with the various users who request new capabilities can keep the Business Analytics Program fresh, responsive, and vibrant over its lifetime. This is part process, people, and culture that need to be introduced as part of the program—and one that can help to achieve greater levels of business alignment and satisfaction with the community of stakeholders. By applying a balance between instilling standards and introducing a process that allows the introduction of new technologies, a continual growth and innovation cycle can be fostered. Standards enable ease of access to licenses that are perceived as "free" (rather than forcing each new member to pay) and reduce barriers to acceptance, while evaluating new technologies that might need introduction into the program increases collaboration and trust between teams.

KEY CONCEPT

> "User adoption grows quickly when licenses, infrastructure, and surrounding processes are in place. It makes it much easier for teams to ramp up projects when they are not hindered by an upfront cost for obtaining licenses or infrastructure, or by having to go through lengthy procurement processes or negotiations. While there are a number of ways to 'chargeback' the BA environment, I'd advocate that it is better treated as an enterprise asset that everyone can benefit from, no different from email. Ensuring the BA technology platform within the program is funded centrally allows for quicker onboarding, helps support standards and enable agility, and ultimately is more cost–effective. While this makes projects cheaper to the business, there are also benefits that can be realized from the ability to develop applications that enable business decisions more quickly."
>
> *—Bill Frank*

Self-Service Processes

Empowering users and allowing easy self-service with technology, training, and expertise that can be leveraged will accelerate adoption quickly. While self-service can often seem risky at first, determining how best to put processes in place that will allow easy self-service is a key to keeping chaos from blooming.

However, while many users ask for self-service, they may require specific tools to feel comfortable with the level of self-service that they need. First, determine what users mean by "self-service":

- Do they want full access to the analytic portfolio or just specific toolsets they can use?
- Why do they require self-service, and what are they looking for?
- What types of self-service would they like to do?

As more users self-serve with tools, analytics reports can become abundant, messy, and hard to manage. Report names and measures may become confusing. Tools such as lineage, glossaries, naming standards, and "gold standard" samples may need to be put in place to obtain consistency as the community grows. In addition, documentation of those trained, who has access to which tools, and regular reports of who is actually using self-service should be captured to get a full view of how self-service is working within the organization.

Enabling Agile Support Processes

It's in the nature of Business Analytics to tie together a variety of information resources. Databases, processes, and platforms are all brought together into a system that reveals the "consistent version of the truth" that management can use. However, developing the necessary metrics that represent this truth is just the technical measure that pulls together the data and processes. On the other hand, keeping that path clear of user problems requires a well-developed and well-publicized path of support. Why? Because if support is fragmented between business units or departments, fixing process problems gets complicated.

> **"The bottom line is that an agile development environment needs an agile support environment to be successful."**
>
> *—John Boyer*

Supporting the Business Analytics Program can be particularly challenging. Multiple databases, multiple platforms, and a variety of technical infrastructures and tools are often supported by a mix of IT departments or business unit entities. Every support element may be surrounded by its own departmental set of processes. As the Business Analytics process extracts data from a variety of databases, there may be a technical mix of software and hardware platforms, different operating systems, and a slew of highly technical steps.

Now consider the user side of the equation: Users need to access these resources for their analytics work, and when problems occur, to whom do they turn for support?

We believe it's essential that your Business Analytics processes monitor how this support is being handled. Simple questions such as "Who is responsible?" and "What is the support process?" must be periodically examined, streamlined, and enhanced. This is especially true in large enterprises when support is regularly scattered between IT, departmental specialists, and tool vendors.

Growing Support Agility

Of course, there is no single simple answer to providing support for complex analytics environments, and we've seen those processes change as the organization matures.

For instance, some early-stage Business Analytics Programs start out with support by individuals who bring a range of skills, often outside the technical IT team. These implementers become expert in their particular analytics infrastructure: *wizards* or *champions* who become adept at resolving user problems. Over time, these individuals begin to manage the variety of infrastructures, tools, and databases that are assembled to deliver the metrics needed by management. As the Business Analytics Program matures, these supporters, wizards, and champions start to converge their talents to provide a broader framework of support.

But where should this support framework reside? Should it be in the IT department? A separate Business Analytics team? Who is responsible for this support framework, and to whom does it report?

Secondarily, how involved should the vendors be in providing support for the various elements in the Business Analytics Program? What about the subsidiaries, business units, or silos within the organization? What role controls this vendor interaction with users across the enterprise?

In other words, who *should* own the ultimate responsibility for supporting the Business Analytics Program? Each organization must solve this dilemma, and—again —no "one size" fits all.

Ultimately having the right mix of a Business Analytics Program office, Analytics Center of Excellence, BICC, or community of practice with defined processes and roles is optimal.

Point of Contact

In our experience, the most successful approach is to establish an easy-to-access *point of contact* for user inquiries and problem solving. This individual or group of individuals will reduce the confusion new users encounter when working through their problems. An easily identifiable point of contact reduces the frustration and steps a user must perform to obtain answers. Frequently asked questions can be centralized and formalized through this point of contact, so that users have a quicker way to obtain the answers they need. Thirdly, the point of contact can spot the difficulties and flaws in the analytics processes more quickly—experiencing the scope of problems as they are uncovered—and can coordinate the responses needed.

Consider also that this easy-to-locate point of contact should handle the relationship with the primary vendors of analytics tools. With this contact point established, the vendors will be able to more quickly focus their support efforts without confusing users or jeopardizing the business relationship. Regardless of how a problem is identified—from user interaction with the tools or through misuse of features within the tools themselves—an established point of contact can orchestrate the organization's response, more quickly investigate remedies, and more accurately communicate the remedies back to the users.

As the Business Analytics Program grows, the support team may ultimately include key members of the IT team, business analysts, and representatives from the user community at large collaborating with vendors. But the value of this point of contact remains significant: It reduces confusion, speeds support, and pushes forward the goals of the program as a whole.

Finally, it's our belief that a periodic review and continual monitoring of the support processes should:

- Provide oversight of the effectiveness of current support processes
- Reduce duplication of effort
- Streamline support responses
- Establish feedback loops to users
- Enable consistent change management processes

By setting up an established point of contact approach for support of the Business Analytics Program, you can:

- Reduce user confusion
- Coordinate vendor interaction and support
- Speed collaborative problem-solving among all elements of the system

Business Analytics Process Design

As the company changes, so too will its processes. One of the most significant elements that should be considered is the strategic and periodic review of the Business Analytics process designs.

The purpose of Business Analytics process design review is to ensure that the elements implemented in the past to propel the Business Analytics Program continue to be appropriate for the organization today. When reviewing processes, key questions to ask include:

- What is the business process that needs to happen?
- How is it done today?
- How can analytics improve it?

All of us have come across projects that no longer make sense or have been made obsolete by newer, more accurate information and methods to derive the information. Yet the metrics may still be in common circulation, confusing the overall picture of the information as a whole.

Analytics process design monitors and directs *how* the Business Analytics Program is being used on the day-to-day level. Does the Business Analytics process still "make sense"? What are the outcomes of the current Business Analytics processes, and do they still match what the organization requires? Are there better ways to measure those outcomes, to plan, or to obtain those results more efficiently? Does the information that is accrued through the Business Analytics Program actually match the outcomes that were anticipated or needed? If not, why not?

By implementing an Analytics Process Review and continually reviewing and monitoring the processes end-to-end—and improving on them—the Business Analytics Program will increase its agility. It will be able to remove steps or programs that are no longer necessary and potentially identify new programs that hold the best opportunities for achieving more accurate results.

> "It is quite common that as an organization grows and matures, multiple processes are put in place that no longer make sense. Sometimes additional processes are put in place to cope with older processes. Examining these business processes end-to-end to determine what makes sense, making improvements, and potentially reengineering them with the addition of new technology can go a long way to maintaining agility and better outcomes."
>
> —*Tracy Harris*

An Agile Business Analytics Process

By now, it should be apparent that building an agile Business Analytics Program is more than installing a shelf of software and instituting a set of standards. It requires a methodology that stresses collaboration between IT and the business functions of the organization to build a community of analytics users who are actively involved in investigating, analyzing, implementing, *and evangelizing* analytics tools toward the goals of the organization. It connects top-level business strategy to the processes that manage the day-to-day operations through to the technologies that support it.

Building the agile Business Analytics Program necessitates the creation of processes that respond dynamically to the organization's needs. These processes bridge the gaps between information silos and firmly establish a collaborative platform with adaptive standards, strong governance, and vibrant educational processes. They require a level of strong management judgment that transcends personality and the culture of the corporation, working with proven agile practices that can intelligently design new analytics processes. Agile Business Analytics also requires some foundational components that facilitate this agility, such as in-house expertise, robust and strategically funded platforms, and licensing options that do not inhibit adoption. An Agile Business Analytics process will examine and challenge preexisting processes if progress toward management goals is at stake. It is a form of adaptive management that is both engineered and incented to bring together people, processes, and systems to activate and energize the strategic policies of decision makers. It's designed to use governance, education, and superior Business Analytics tools to form a broad coalition of collaboration between business activists and technical experts.

Clearly, developing an agile Business Analytics process is a challenging task, but it's one that can deliver superior results to the organization, empower its users to excellence, and help drive the business toward its strategic goals.

The next few pages present a case study in process development and improvement— and how improvements in process can enhance business outcomes. We then take a deeper dive into how to look at your processes and program to determine how to stay continually agile and open to change. Next, we will move on to the final key to Business Analytics Program success, and one of the most important: the technology consideration behind making Business Analytics work.

Case Study on Process:
Daimler Trucks North America

From guest author Thomas J. Marks, Continuous Improvement
Process Manager, DaimlerTrucks North America LLC

***Business Analytics cut order-to-build times,
boosted quality and serviceability, and reduced costs***

> "Through our relentless focus on quality and customer service, we've been
> able to weather a difficult economic period without making significant
> layoffs and maintain our lead in North American market share. In large
> part, this has been made possible by the adoption of lean manufacturing
> principles, powered by analytics."
>
> *—Thomas J. Marks, Continuous Improvement Process Manager,*
> *DaimlerTrucks North America LLC*

Daimler Overview

Daimler Trucks North America LLC (DTNA)—a Daimler company—is the largest
heavy-duty truck manufacturer in North America and a leading producer of medium-duty
trucks, specializing in commercial vehicles. The company—and its affiliates—employs
16,000 people and manufactures nearly 100,000 customized vehicles a year.

When the company understood that new emissions regulations were creating a
unique cycle of fluctuating customer demand, it began a new strategy to maintain its
leading market share in the NAFTA region. That strategy focused on enhancing truck
quality and customer service through a process of continuous improvement.

According to ASQ, a global quality community (*http://asq.org*), continuous improvement process (CIP, or CI) is defined as "an ongoing effort to improve products, services,
or processes." This effort can seek "incremental" improvement over time or "break-
through" improvement all at once. At Daimler Trucks, the customer-valued processes
became a key strategic focus: They are constantly evaluated and improved in the light
of their efficiency, effectiveness, and flexibility.

To accomplish these strategies, DTNA needed to:

- Strengthen the company's commitment to customer service and quality
- Enhance the agility and adaptability of the business to meet the unique
  challenges of changing economic conditions and emissions regulations
- Change the company focus to an analytics-driven culture for continuous
  improvement

Daimler began by mapping out its entire "customer to cash" value stream, which covered all business processes—from the initial customer order, through the design and build stages, on to fulfillment and payment. This value stream map enabled the company to examine processes within its business and to define a baseline for achieving the goals of continuous improvement.

Then Daimler set up a Business Excellence Department to govern Lean Six Sigma, a methodology that helped DTNA identify the metrics needed to drive the company's performance. The company established a performance management office (PMO) as a component of that department, tasked with creating performance guidelines by using Lean Six Sigma. Each year, the company's executives defined the business goals, and the PMO helped to match appropriate metrics to each goal.

Daimler Trucks then utilized its analytics program to track and monitor those metrics via analytics dashboards and scorecards for each relevant team of employees. The HR department became responsible for performance management as it pertains to individuals' goals, and the analytics processes show the measured performance against each metric. As the performance measurement became more widely understood, employees began to take individual responsibility for their performance. In addition, a series of internal processes had to be put in place to support the data-driven culture, train the employees to design and use metrics, and maintain momentum in the organization.

For example, analytics dashboards provided the COO and the plant managers with daily feedback into the operational performance of each element, highlighting areas that could be improved. Today each plant, department, and team can see its current performance on a live scorecard.

The adoption of analytics and the continuous improvement culture began to pervade every area of the enterprise, from the production line, supply chain, and quality management through to supporting departments such as finance, purchasing, sales, marketing, IT, and after-sales servicing.

Meanwhile, the constant visibility of analytics data—reinforced by the creation of events such as the company's "Continuous Improvement Day" and regular processes annually and throughout the year to revisit improvement areas and processes designed to create continuous improvement—helped employees at every level of the business to focus on both meeting immediate targets and working toward overall improvements in the longer term.

> "The visual tools that our Business Analytics environment provides have enabled everyone in the organization to engage and focus on continuous improvement."
>
> —*Thomas J. Marks*

Best Practices in Processes

As a result, the combination of Business Analytics technologies, processes, and Lean Six Sigma methodologies has enabled every area of the business—not just manufacturing—to focus on continuous improvement. Best practices that contributed to this success include:

- ✓ **Involving the right stakeholders who will support processes:** The CIP initiatives and the analytics program at Daimler Trucks were initiated and supported by the company's top-level executives.
- ✓ **Putting processes in place that allow initiatives to break down silos:** Daimler Trucks understood that a successful initiative starts with goal-setting and that performance monitoring should apply not only to manufacturing but across various areas of the business—including finance, purchasing, supply chain, and quality management, as well as after-sales services.
- ✓ **Continually examining and improving processes to maintain and increase adoption:** The adoption of Business Analytics allowed the team to put in place processes that would enable teams to align the company's information with its lean manufacturing and lean office CIP strategies. It enabled the company to map out its entire "value stream" and assess the areas where specific improvement projects would deliver the greatest value. Then, on a day-to-day basis, Business Analytics provided the visibility into the performance of each plant, department, and team, encouraging all employees to take personal responsibility for driving the goals of continuous improvement.

Proven Business Benefits

By setting the right balance between achievable short-term goals and targeted long-term improvements, the company transformed its culture and began moving in a more customer-valued direction:

- Daimler increased its responsiveness to customer demand by reducing order-to-build times through process improvements—from deeper supply chain analytics to customer-to-cash.
- The CI process reduced exceptions per order by 40 percent by identifying potential component sourcing issues before they affected the build process. This meant more vehicles met the client's exact specifications.
- Analytics helped increase product quality, reducing early warranty claims (claims in the first 30 days of use) by 50 percent.
- The CI process increased the organization's focus on serviceability: Daimler's repair processes are now recognized as best-in-class, with a repair time 50 percent faster than the competition.
- Analytics helped optimize Daimler's dealer repair process, cutting the cost of repairs for vehicles under warranty by 37 percent.

> "Our commitment to driving quality through analytics is recognized throughout the manufacturing sector and across the state. Our facility in Cleveland, North Carolina, won *Quality Magazine*'s large plant of the year award, and our CEO was recently named Oregon's most admired executive by the *Portland Business Journal*."
>
> —*Thomas J. Marks*

Daimler Trucks' commitment to its Business Analytics program has enabled it not only to identify key focus areas for improvement but also to *measure* the tangible results from its CI processes. Without a strong program designed with processes that will help maintain momentum and continually improve the program that has been put in place, these levels of success would not have been achieved.

Adding Up the Business Value

Table 5 summarizes the benefits and impacts of Daimler Trucks' new analytics system.

Business area	Benefits	Business impact
Meeting customer demand	Accelerated the order-to-build process	
Quality management	Reduced warranty claims within first 30 days	50%
	Reduced exceptions per order	40%
After-sales service	Led the industry in turnaround time for repairs for over-the-road vehicle types	50% faster than industry average
	Reduced overall costs in the repair process	37%

Table 5: Results Achieved with Daimler Trucks' Analytics System

CIP and Business Analytics Equals Better Customer Satisfaction

The careful and deliberate use of Business Analytics has empowered Daimler Trucks to steer successfully through a difficult economic period for the North American automotive industry. One result was that the company faced fewer challenges in terms of layoffs and financial problems than many of its competitors faced.

Today, as truck demand returns to the market, Daimler Trucks uses the CIP and analytics processes to extend its focus on quality to attract new customer orders and streamline its production, enabling the organization to deliver increased financial performance in the coming years with greater customer satisfaction.

When the economics of heavy-duty truck manufacturing and sales became challenging, Daimler Trucks executed a strategy of continuous improvement to enhance the quality of its products, improve customer service, and increase customer satisfaction. Its Business Analytics Program energized the strategy and delivered the critical systems that helped the organization achieve its goals.

Practical Tips:
How to Keep Business Analytics Processes Agile

Business Analytics Program agility is composed of agility in two main areas: methodology and program deployment as well as technology and development agility (Figure 26).

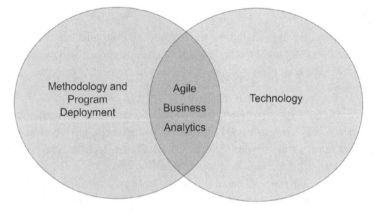

Figure 26: Components of Agile Business Analytics

Methodology and program deployment are made up of a combination of the way a program is designed and executed and include the following considerations as examples.

Strategy & Value

- Can your team rapidly reprioritize when strategy changes? How quickly can you understand priorities and satisfy new business demands? How connected are you to the business strategy? To stakeholder engagement?
- How quickly do you react? Do you just react or are you looped in and proactive to solve business needs?
- Are you providing value to the teams? Do you have champions who will promote your help? Is it push vs. pull?
- How do you prioritize projects? Is there executive involvement?

People & Process

- Do you have an organizational structure that is purely IT, purely business, or a mix of both?
- How do you communicate? Just by submitting requirements or through iterative discussions? Do you bring teams together?
- Are you promoting and empowering self-service?
- Process and governance: Are you hindering usage or having people escape to other means?

- Are you working in small projects with greater self-service or on a bigger program scope that is holding units in line?

Connections and collaboration between the various stakeholders will ensure that as needs change, the program can respond. By reviewing the processes that are put in place end-to-end, you can better determine where the breakdowns are occurring and hindering the program.

From a technology perspective, how the technology is architected, what capabilities individuals have access to, and how technology is introduced will also increase or hinder agility. We discuss considerations in this area further in the next chapter; however, some of them include:

- Have you built your Business Analytics platform and infrastructure to solve both the needs of IT (consistency, information management, governance, security) and the needs of the business (access to data, cross-departmental collaboration, quick-start projects, rapid development, self-service)?
- Do you have the range of capabilities available to allow for self-service with a variety of tools to ensure you are not turning away individuals or having them create another silo in the organization?
- Are you ready with your technology? Can you deliver rapid licenses, grow quickly, and allow for fast project starts? How is your solution architected to grow, scale, onboard new projects, and introduce new data? Is it open and do you deal with it early enough so you are not just reacting?
- Do you have a mechanism to always proactively be evaluating and introducing new technologies or features and be innovative, or do you deliver just a strict, single, one-size-fits-all standard? Have you implemented technology with a variety of capabilities? Are you thinking about innovative deployment options?

As you assess your program, here are some practical tips to keep in mind today to ensure you maintain agility in your program:

- Develop the mindset of keeping agile and continually changing, and share it with your peers and executives.
- Talk to your champions:
  - Become self-aware of their daily problems and how they view you. Are you pushing or pulling? Don't just react to change; be involved in change.
  - Ask your clients why they might not be using the tools. Open the communication, and work together on a common problem.

- Assess which processes slow you down the most:

  ◦ Question your processes. Determine why each one is important, and cut out what is not.

  ◦ Keep in mind that being agile doesn't mean "no process"; it means collaborative process.

- How can you innovate today? Determine one business innovation that will delight your partners.
- Plan for change—agile is about constantly meeting the needs of the changing business, and you need to plan for it.

Keeping agile and being able to innovate and respond to change quickly will establish trust and partnership with the community of users and help to continually improve the program throughout the journey.

Process Checklist

In the "Process" chapter, we discussed several program areas to consider for your Business Analytics Program to implement a suitable set of processes that will create efficiencies while maintaining agility. Use this checklist to see which areas might be useful to integrate and manage over time in your organization:

- ✓ Are the contacts in the Analytics Center of Excellence or the team responsible for analytics initiatives easy to find and identify?
- ✓ Do you have a knowledge repository and best practice sharing area where members of the organization can get clear understanding, direction, and help on how to engage in the program?
- ✓ Are your onboarding processes outlined?
- ✓ Do you have enablement and adoption programs in place?
- ✓ Do you have a communication process established that shares news and information and constantly brings users together to collaborate?
- ✓ Do you have an advise and consult framework to establish how you can empower users?
- ✓ Are your requirements-gathering processes collaborative and outcome-based, or are they technical specifications that solution before understanding the demands?
- ✓ Are your development processes iterative, or do they take a waterfall approach that limits communication?
- ✓ Are you connected closely with a data governance program where you can share best practices and integrate them into the program?
- ✓ Do you have standards in place and the ability to deliver licenses quickly to onboard new teams?
- ✓ Do you encourage self-service and have processes in place that will create success?
- ✓ Do you have support in place for users who need assistance?
- ✓ Do you review business processes regularly to understand how you can continually improve both business and overall business analytics program processes?

Chapter 5
Key #5: Technology

In the preceding chapters, we discussed many of the "softer" elements of a Business Analytics Program and how they can impact success. The foundation of a Business Analytics Program is the technology itself. However, to ensure business outcomes are achieved by meeting the needs of users, technology selection should be based on these earlier elements—which is why we left technology as the last "Key" to program success.

Business Analytics technologies include capabilities that span tools that support Business Intelligence, what-if scenario planning, predictive analytics, budgeting, forecasting, performance and financial management capabilities, and risk management solutions. They also include the technologies that capture, extract, manage, and govern the information used for these applications. Given the diverse set of solutions that could be architected to create a whole solution, there is no single technology strategy that is a silver bullet for every organization. An organization has many factors to consider when architecting the right business solution and technology infrastructure required for a successful Business Analytics Program—from Business Analytics maturity, to identifying existing technologies that can be leveraged, to understanding which individuals in the organization need to use the various tools in an effective and efficient way. When considering technology choices, several common elements should be considered:

- Types of analytic capabilities, including Business Intelligence, predictive modeling, data mining, text mining, statistical analytics, in-memory analytics, what-if scenario planning, search-based analytics, visualization, budgeting, forecasting, planning, and risk analytics. The organization needs to define its taxonomy around analytics, the user cases for each type, and standards for each capability that can be used.
- Growth and change over time, and the need to be flexible with the full stack of technologies that enable Business Analytics—from system and manual data sources, to Information Management (master, meta, and dimensional data), to data architecture and database platforms, to analytics capabilities that span

from reports to predictive tools and varying delivery capabilities as well as supporting practices. Potential masses of information—or "big data"—that the Business Analytics Program will be using over time require consideration of the technologies that can impact performance (e.g., SMP vs. MPP vs. in-memory options, hardware vendors, data security).

- Deployment options, such as enterprise software, cloud computing, and others.
- An understanding of overall cost of ownership and the investment roadmap.
- The ability to create, access, reach, leverage, cleanse, and profile information across the organization as it grows to result in improved insight.

> **"One-size-fits-all technology approaches are like one-size-fits-all dresses. They actually will only ever really satisfy a subset of clients."**
>
> *—John Boyer*

In short, the outcome of the choices that are made need to support varying types of decision makers while also protecting and leveraging IT investments and especially understanding how to grow infrastructure for the future (portfolio planning). The infrastructures that support each enterprise, or even each department in an enterprise, may be very different. The tools deployed could be varied and diverse and possibly at odds with standardization and rationalization strategies. User communities are as varied and diverse as the organizations themselves, and a "one-size-fits-all" approach will likely result in a suboptimal capability profile. In addition, new requirements and new technologies arrive with amazing rapidity and can be disruptive to in-place strategies. Investigating and integrating these elements into our current architecture and processes can pose real and continual challenges. In this chapter, we deep-dive into these areas and discuss:

- The impact of Business Analytics maturity on technology strategy
- Technology decisions:
  - To standardize or not to standardize?
  - To build or buy?
- Considerations for Business Analytics technology strategy evolution:
  - Evolving business user capability requirements
  - Business Analytics and Information Management maturity
  - User adoption and organic growth
  - Deployment considerations
  - Innovation
  - Strategy successes and failures

Business Analytics is a subject that impacts the entire enterprise. How we address both the requirements of the enterprise and the prerequisites of technology will require vibrant, adaptive, and resilient strategies. These strategies will prioritize the needs of

management through Business Analytics and the requirements of continuity, performance, and security for the enterprise as a whole.

Understanding Business Analytics Technology Maturity

If we again take the Analytics Quotient Maturity Model as an example, we can see how
organizations mature with technology in their programs. As organizations grow in their
sophistication with Business Analytics, there's a misperception that the complexity of
user interactions will also always grow.

Organizations might start their Business Analytics journeys with simple tools, such
as spreadsheets, and move through an array of services and tools in the quest for more
information, increased performance, and better metrics to drive the business strategy.
The evolution of a Business Analytics Program also often leads organizations through
multiple data stores, data marts, data warehouses, arrays of software tools, hardware
servers, and an infrastructure that increases in complexity as it delivers the important
information ever more quickly for the demands of users.

Along with this increasing burden of infrastructure come increased infrastructure
costs of maintenance and support, as well as a potential lack of agility to adapt to new
challenges as the recognition of the mission-critical nature of the system grows.

These challenges require a technology strategy that recognizes that it will need to
grow and change over time, as well as consideration about how to build it with openness
and flexibility in mind. As new users present new challenges and opportunities, the
program will need to adapt and be ready to evolve with open communication and flexibility to evaluate and understand how to adapt to business changes with a view to offering
a scalable and innovative strategy that is constantly reviewed over time with a view to
the future. Keeping in mind that the goal is integration and interconnectivity, viewing
information across all time horizons (past, present, and future) and potentially embedding
analytics in business processes to increase efficiencies and time to respond can allow your
program to move more quickly toward innovation and higher maturity levels.

To Standardize or Not to Standardize?

This is a question that organizations eventually ask as they mature toward a higher level
of analytics sophistication. Rationalization of tools and creation of standards offer many
benefits, such as reducing total cost of ownership. However, we have found that it is
not necessarily standardization on a single tool (providing a one-size-fits-all Business
Analytics strategy approach) that offers the highest benefit, but a set of standards that
offers quick and easy access to available licenses, sharing of skills, best practices, expertise, and the ability to be agile and flexible to easily onboard new analytics projects and
initiatives. What standardization should not reflect is a closed, authoritative approach
to dictating a single narrow tool that might not meet the diverse needs of the enterprise.
With this thought in mind, we will discuss how to evolve a Business Analytics strategy to
achieve a balance between defining standards and achieving both the goals of IT and the
business in that balance.

> "A technology plan should not be developed in a vacuum. What do the various parts of the business need? What are the expectations? What are the IT requirements? We've seen many times where business and IT talk only when there are problems or specific dependencies. There needs to be a formal partnership and an understanding/alignment and evolution on short- and long-term planning."
>
> —Bill Frank

The decision to create a set of standards and to centralize Business Analytics technology infrastructure depends on the maturity level of the organization in its analytic culture. The move from a diverse set of capabilities to a centralized license management and infrastructure environment is one that should be done with various key stakeholders at the decision point. Understanding the capabilities that the organization requires and discussing the value of standardization to ensure it can still meet the objectives of the business and promote efficiency of the IT team is an exercise that involves assessment of the current capabilities and business requirements and a shared understanding of the overall objectives between the various teams to ensure that business needs are not sacrificed but that increased gains in reuse of information and reduced cost are also understood.

When considering implementing standards, the following questions need to be on the table:

- What is the reason for the standardization (e.g., cost reduction, training synergy, resource sharing)?
- What capabilities exist that are successfully being used?
- What capabilities do the various users require?
- Which technologies are easily integrated, extended, and reused? How do these align with your overall Information Management architecture?
- How and where can you sunset technologies and easily transition to standards?
- Which technologies provide scalability as the program grows? What business needs may be on the horizon that should be considered now (i.e., mobile devices, integration with social media, big data, and so on)?
- What skill sets exist in-house to support the technology?

Previous chapters discussed the benefits of creating standards, from encouraging adoption, improving total cost of ownership, and reducing the amount of training, management, and processes as well as creating and driving a culture of understood analytics throughout the organization.

To Build or Buy?

As a program grows, there may be requirements for which it appears to be more practical to apply custom solutions vs. a prepackaged solution to fill the need. It may be easy to implement a custom solution in a short period of time, but weighing the positives and negatives in a build vs. buy analysis are very important to long-term project success.

While today's short-term need to solve an immediate challenge may make a custom solution appear cost-effective, understanding the long-term possibilities of a project are important in order to get a better sense of the total cost of the solution and future development. To assist in weighing the benefits of build vs. buy decisions, you need to understand short-term and long-term costs and benefits of possible decisions.

Table 6 provides a sample chart you can use to compare solutions for a new project.

Criteria	Option 1	Option 2	Option 3
Description	Out-of-the-box functionality of corporate tool	Enhanced functionality of tool through customization	Custom development, short-term, quick hit
Integration with existing platform and infrastructure	100%	75%	50%
Compatible with future convergence	Yes	Yes	No
Meets business requirements	75%	100%	100%
Can deliver on promises made to client	Most	No (delayed by 1 month)	Yes
Scalability	Highly scalable	Highly scalable	Less scalable
Time to deliver	4 months	10 months	3 months
Cost	$500K	$750K	$350K
Cross-sell opportunities	Medium	Very strong	None
Aligns with corporate strategic direction	Yes	Yes	No
Additional phase flexibility	Some	Yes	Yes

Table 6: Comparing Solutions for a New Project

While in many cases short-term costs may seem like a reason to build a custom solution, long-term viability and costs need to be considered before moving forward with this type of strategy. Weigh the benefits carefully, and ensure you make the best choice before embarking on a new project.

Evolving a BA Technology Strategy

> "Whether it is evolving an existing technology through an upgrade or introducing a new capability, organizations need to plan for rapid change in technology and user requirements. Keeping fresh, innovative and up-to-date will inspire teams and keep the program fresh over time in addition to ensuring individuals have the tools they need to succeed."
>
> *—Tracy Harris*

As we discussed, Business Analytics Programs can and should change over time, reflecting new business information and analysis requirements, new deployment options, the continued growth in users, enhanced capabilities to existing platform, and new technology capabilities.

Meanwhile, technologies don't necessarily disappear as the new arrives. The technology challenge is more than building a robust Business Analytics infrastructure based on a one-time architecture exercise; it's also about recognizing that the architecture and infrastructure must evolve along with the business requirements and the marketplace to meet both current and future demands. We must have a technology strategy to address these realities.

Let's examine four factors we feel underpin our technology strategies:

- Business strategy requirements evolution
- Growing user adoption levels
- Deployment strategies
- Disruptive technologies

Business Strategy Requirements Evolution

When asked "What is the most critical issue to address when deploying a successful Business Analytics solution?" BA organizations in a recent survey[1] said that their number one priority was "meeting business users' timelines and expectations." But placing that priority within the separate contexts of evolving business requirements, changing technologies, corporate growth, organizational mergers, and the hundreds of other variables that are vying for our attention, we're constantly challenging the Business Analytics technical infrastructure.

> "One of the greatest challenges faced by IT is the significant maturity of business teams in utilizing and understanding technology. Business users are keenly aware of tools, and they often want them but are not always sure how they will use them. They may also not understand the realities of necessary internal IT processes (e.g., procurement, negotiations, engineering, architecture) that appear to slow down users' ability to acquire and deploy new tools.
>
> "While a technology with the promise of QUICK deployment with NO IT needed may seem like it will meet their needs, over time the realization occurs that it isn't always the best long-term solution and it may cost more in the long run. A good Business Analytics Program allows for existing capabilities to be understood and new capabilities to be marketed, and it helps the business understand the sometimes complex but necessary IT involvement. IT should try as much as possible to build in process agility, facilitate proofs of concept, and be proactive in understanding the ever-changing technology landscape."
>
> —*Bill Frank*

---

[1] "Lifecycle Management Survey." IBM, July 2011.

What we need is a strategy that acknowledges the organizational flux and business requirements and addresses the changing environment without drifting too far from our primary goals. Capability selection is not done without collaboration based on user needs and outcomes. Mapping business goals to capabilities and helping to select the right tools that meet user needs is crucial. This may include introducing the "art of the possible" to users who have limited experience in analytics, helping them to understand the various time horizons that can be viewed with analytics (past, present, and future), and developing a clear understanding of how they need to view and work with the data and information.

One strategy we have found useful is establishing domain areas that segment the enterprise's analytic needs along line-of-business requirements.

Line-of-Business Domain Model to Improve Technology Selection and Implementation

In a Line-of-Business (LOB) Domain model, each line of business is deeply involved in helping to develop and maintain its own business strategy alignments within the larger corporate business strategy as part of the Center of Excellence design. In many cases, satellite Centers of Excellence may be developed that work closely with the main Center of Excellence team. This type of organization requires executive sponsorship of the domain and management representation within individual Business Analytics Steering Committees. It also requires strong role definitions and communication ties with any centralized team that can manage across domains.

The Line-of-Business Domain area establishes a steering committee or "change" board that is managed through the Center of Excellence program and community to develop its own Business Analytics project priorities, yet work to embrace an analytic architecture using a set of standards defined by the Analytics Center of Excellence. This committee would also be responsible for monitoring the progress of individual projects.

The structure functions as follows:

- The LOB Domain Steering Committee aligns the enterprise business strategy with its individual LOB requirements, identifying the metrics that need to flow upward to the enterprise decision makers.

> "Keep in mind that the LOB domains may be at different levels of maturity and that a staggered approach is acceptable. However, the technical architecture should keep cross-domain analytical capabilities in mind when selecting data models, warehousing, and BA tools."
>
> —*Brian Green*

- The Domain's requirements create the "demand flow" to the appropriate IT experts. It assigns business personnel to the Business Analytics project management team to work with IT representatives.
- IT builds the required data warehouse and the pipelines of the necessary components to deliver the information to the individual LOB Domains projects (master data, metadata, business rules, packaged analytics elements, and so on).

This approach can allow for more flexible delivery and involvement from the business side while establishing roles and responsibilities for each team. However, it can also lead to chaos if open dialogue about standards and requirements does not take place.

> "A common mistake is that the LOB and the enterprise team have not established a steering committee within the Center of Excellence structure or governance process and try to bolt this on after a time when they start to run into conflicts or the LOB starts to drift away from the enterprise BA strategy. For the LOB method to be successful, the establishment of these elements is necessary and needs to be defined early in the lifecycle of the BA program."
>
> —*Kay Van De Vanter*

How about when the enterprise's business strategy changes? How does the LOB Domain respond?

When the organization's business strategy changes—or when opportunities present themselves to streamline the overall business processes—the LOB Domain representatives meet with the organization's senior executives to identify the new goals, and the new potential projects, keeping their overall Business Analytics architecture model in mind. A representative from IT, reporting to the CIO and charged with sustaining the enterprise data management infrastructure, is also part of these discussions, identifying potential technical solutions in consultation. As a project strategy is developed, the LOB Domain Steering Committee spearheads the execution using the resources of IT.

The key to this LOB Domain structure is the required and continual alignment of the Business Analytics technical infrastructure with the business strategies that the key decision makers need.
KEY CONCEPT

Ultimately, the LOB Domain Steering Committee identifies the project requirements and the priorities that impact its domain, and the Business Analytics and IT project management team determines the best solution to meet the goals. This "top-down/bottoms-up" structure helps to ensure that business strategy alignment is maintained in a coordinated fashion using the methods and processes that the organization's Analytics Center of Excellence can support. At the same time, the LOB Domain ensures that its day-to-day requirements are incorporated into the overall planning.

Architecting for User Adoption and Growth

A recent survey by IBM of Business Analytics organizations indicated that the adoption levels of Business Analytics tools by users was one of the *most significant measures* of Business Analytics success. The logic is straight-forward: If the community of users is growing, the system is being adequately utilized. However, growing user adoption levels can also have a significant impact on the technology infrastructure. These impacts include:

- License fee costs
- Server infrastructure and resource capacity
- Performance and scalability
- Business Analytics and IT support and training costs
- Internal competencies (people to do the engineering, design, build, and support work)

A balance needs to be struck between what users will accept and what the infrastructure can sustain. But how do you track this delicate balance?

> "A governance process that works with the business organizations and IT to ensure there is a clear understanding of the capacity level of the infrastructure and a forward look into the expected usage so growth can be planned is necessary. Planning for infrastructure growth is a not a quick turnaround item, so a means to forecast demand and a clear understanding of the capacity of the existing infrastructure is needed."
>
> —*John Boyer*

Many Business Analytics Programs use their own methodologies to monitor how the user community is making use of the tools provided. What does this mean?

If, by reviewing usage statistics, the Business Analytics team determines that a series of reports are being run an inordinate number of times, it should interview the user to determine why the activity is so high. Then, it can investigate how the user's processes can be streamlined or improved to reduce high rates of usage.

Often, the user doesn't understand that the same information may be provided in a better, more consolidated manner through a different, existing vehicle that utilizes fewer resources. This may be a simple issue of providing adequate training.

On the other hand, some organizations consume high levels of resources to yield close-to-real-time results for daily or even hourly processes. The LOB organization may demand this level of usage, even though these processes detrimentally affect network and data warehouse performance.

The Analytics Center of Excellence can study these scenarios to implement better utilization models, staging less frequently accessed data into more concise masters and performing ETLs during off-hour processing.

This is *architecting* the data warehouse for optimal results, and it can deliver substantial savings while preserving close-to-real-time performance for the user.

Some organizations monitor usage to identify where Business Analytics tool licenses are *under-utilized.* In IBM's recent "Lifecycle Management" survey[2], 46 percent of participants indicated that license fee costs created the greatest impact on the total cost of ownership of their Business Analytics environments. So, monitoring under-utilized licenses can make a significant impact on lowering TCO and increasing the company's ROI.

When these organizations spot little or no activity in the use of the Business Analytics tool and then connect that usage level with the silos, divisions, or individuals to which they are assigned, they should investigate. If the tool no longer meets the users' needs, the software may be removed or the license reassigned to other areas of the organization. The Business Analytics Project Team can reevaluate how the tool should be used in the particular sector or silo and then provide the necessary training and support to maximize the value of the tool.

Monitoring user licenses can be a particular boon to the organization that is following a "shared services" model: It reduces overall licensing costs for the entire organization while leveraging the tool's use to increase ROI and decrease TCO. Monitoring and removing licenses that are not being utilized should also follow your IT security guidelines. Many organizations require the revoking of a license and password if it has not been accessed within a specific number of days.

Regardless of the techniques used to track and monitor user adoption levels, these levels remain a key metric by which an organization can measure successful implementations or spot areas of weakness where efficiencies are suffering. With experience, the Business Analytics technical team can learn how to architect, predict, and ensure the successes of the Business Analytics infrastructure, so that new Business Analytics projects can better meet the needs of the enterprise as a whole.

Confidence in Information

A major factor in driving user adoption is having high confidence in the data. While this book does not dive deep into the Information Management level of the conversation, it needs to be recognized that this aspect is as crucial as the analytics infrastructure itself. The ability to capture the right data, integrate it, ensure it is of good quality, and access and store it will either make or break the success of the overall program. This point

---

[2] Ibid.

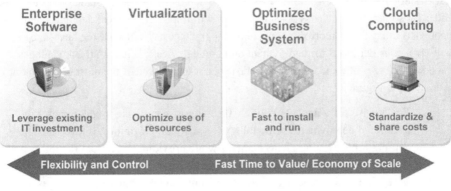

Figure 27: Deployment Options

demonstrates the requirement for having the Information Management team as a key group in the Center of Excellence design. Close and constant collaboration with this team must be maintained throughout the program journey.

Increasing confidence in data typically requires three areas of consideration:

- **Understanding:** Understanding the definitions around the data and the lineage of where it came from
- **Trust:** The ability to properly integrate, profile, cleanse, and de-duplicate data to inspire trust
- **Relevance:** The ability to access the right data based on security entitlements to get a relevant view of the world

Including Information Management as part of the deployment strategy and Center of Excellence team and establishing clear roles and responsibilities between business and IT in the many Information Management responsibilities will assist in achieving earlier success.

Deployment Approaches

In the aforementioned "Lifecycle Management" survey[3], 47 percent of BA organizations indicated that a crucial element to their technology strategy is how the Business Analytics deployment fits the organization's overall IT deployment strategy. Research has shown that traditional on-premise software installation or private clouds prevail as the dominant methods for Business Analytics deployment. However, alternative deployment approaches are rapidly taking root and gaining adherents.

IT and business management executives need to ask critical questions to determine the best method for their Business Analytics deployment: Which approach represents the

---

[3] Ibid.

best strategy for my organization? Does any one deployment method stand out as a clear leader for solving the business pressures? How will it impact Business Analytics deployment costs today and tomorrow? What about upgrade costs? What are the near- and long-term considerations for deployment on mobile devices? What are the advantages and disadvantages of each approach? Let's take a look at some of the most common ones, as depicted in Figure 27.

- **Enterprise software**: Quite often, the enterprise software model remains the traditional deployment methodology for many organizations. It leverages the corporation's existing IT investments while providing maximum flexibility and control over how our infrastructure is built.

- **Virtualization:** Some organizations continue to investigate opportunities to reduce server costs through the use of virtualization technologies that share the physical hardware resources of servers and networks while sustaining the values of separate Business Analytics environments. However, concerns about security and workload performance bottlenecks sometimes weigh heavily on the minds of larger organizations' IT decision makers. This is a rapidly evolving technology, and many organizations have a combination of Enterprise and Virtualization. These options are not mutually exclusive, and they can be used effectively together to provide robust Business Analytics environments at reduced cost.

- **Optimized business systems:** Organizations may want to consider optimized business systems for startup Business Analytics operations because they're fast to install and provide basic business analytic tools to meet the most common Business Analytics requirements. However, as user adoption levels increase and the BA organization grows, optimized business systems may require customization to continue to meet the needs of the corporation. Multiple optimized systems, distributed among divisions or silos, will still need to coordinated, and while the initial setup may be quick, the flexibility to connect data warehouses into a "consistent version of the truth" for management may add complexity and delay the progress of projects. Still, optimized business systems are a great, cost-effective way to establish a baseline architecture.

- **Public vs. private cloud:** Cloud deployments are becoming more common. Overall, cloud deployments can enable agility, improve time to deployment, and even allow the ability to sandbox or prototype analytics projects quickly. *Public Cloud* BA implementations offer prebuilt Business Analytics standards and incredible economies of scale. However, the requirements of your organization's security and the reliability of cloud services may require consideration when investigating this particular deployment option. Meanwhile cloud deployments offer great advantages to the new BA organization, and some of our enterprises deploy *Private Cloud* services to help us manage costs and increase efficiencies for distributed divisions or silos.

The main point here is that deployment options are at the center of the BA infrastructure strategy, and while new technologies are rapidly maturing, concerns for flexibility, control, throughput, and security will always rise to the top of the decision-making process.

Innovation

Like many Business Analytics professionals, when we get together to discuss technology opportunities, the one discussion that recurs is innovation disruption and Business Analytics agility.

On the one hand, our Analytics Centers of Excellence are tasked with establishing the supportable standards and best practices necessary to feed the demands of the enterprise business strategy. These standards and best practices are necessary to provide adequate support to users, streamline implementations, and reduce costs.

On the other hand, our organizations need to be agile in their response with newer technologies—both software- and hardware-based technologies. Some of today's most promising technologies for analytics include:

- **Mobile:** Business users want analytics on the go. Tablet devices and smart phones are much more sophisticated today and offer information anytime, anywhere. How can analytics be offered in the most compelling ways to use on mobile devices? Interaction with information can also be different on mobile devices with limited size and touchscreen flexibility, so innovative thinking and development will be required to deliver analytics in the way that is most useful to these devices.
- **Big data:** Big data offers the opportunity to explore information that may not have been accessible or manageable before. This requires new thinking and innovation around capturing and working with large amounts of data. It also offers new opportunities to explore new areas that may not have been considered in the past. Working with business users to determine the high-value opportunities and how best they can be captured needs to be considered.
- **Visualization:** As more business users begin to use the tools, visually appealing graphics and exploration tools become a necessity. Innovative thinking about how best to offer visual appeal and the toolsets that can provide the flexibility required for visualization without too much confusion or clutter needs to be factored into an analytics program.
- **Cloud:** We mentioned the cloud as a deployment option earlier in this chapter, but we feel that cloud needs to be considered again within the topic of innovation. It has the promise of faster access, speedier development, and flexibility for users that needs to be considered.

However, many of these technologies require new considerations to make them suitable for deployment in an enterprise BA infrastructure. Items of concern include:

- **Security:** Does the solution meet the basic security requirements established by the Business Analytics Program Office? Does it provide independent authentication and authorization?
- **Compliance:** How does the solution relate to regulation and compliance requirements established outside the program?
- **Deployment:** Does the solution fit into the realm of deployment options that IT and the program can support?
- **Configurability:** Will the solution configure to meet the needs of other Business Analytics users and the overall requirements of the infrastructure?
- **Performance:** Will the solution provide high performance and satisfy the needs of the users?

We are firm believers that the Business Analytics Program needs to have a mechanism to continually monitor new offerings, but that this analysis should be thorough and well managed and should meet criteria for inclusion in the standard approved by the program. It should also align to a known, identified, or developing business need.

The guidelines for initiating R&D investigation into a new technology are simple:

- It must significantly add value to the business.
- It must fill a gap in the existing Business Analytics Program capability.
- It must offer substantial potential for reducing or offsetting cost.
- It must offer a clear opportunity for increasing performance.
- There must be a secure method that improves delivery.
- It is an observed deviation from the standard platform that is in full use and is experiencing strong usage and should be evaluated.

But to handle the impact of new technologies that may be disruptive to your current Business Analytics Program, it's important to understand how these technologies will impact the BA infrastructure through each of its maturity phases.

Technology Growth and Maturity

A recent IBM survey of Business Analytics users identified that the ease of use, extensibility of technology, and manageability and scalability of the selected BA solutions are clear concerns of BA organizations[4].

However, achieving and maintaining this level of technological maturity is clearly an ongoing endeavor. Software additions and upgrades ripple through the organizations' infrastructures on a seemingly never-ending cycle; new business requirements cascade

---

[4] IBM/Cognos Survey of BICC Sites. IBM/Cognos, 2011.

through the organization; user demands for training and support are continuous. Unless we can place our organizations into a context of growth and maturity, it will be difficult to gauge our progress and devise the strategies that meet the challenges ahead.

This also means the technical team, as adoptions grows in the organization, needs to consider the impact of new development, performance, upgrades, and administration of the toolsets. Often, business users don't want to hear about many of these concerns; technology should appear seamless—it should just work. However, this is not always the case. Technology in early stages usually requires testing. As it grows, it potentially requires new hardware to support additional users, and as technology improves, upgrades are often necessary. Therefore, processes to evaluate, communicate, and inform team members of these new additions are necessary.

For upgrade specifically, you may have different teams who have various business needs that should not be interrupted at a certain time of the year. Therefore, plan with your teams when upgrades will take place and schedule them so they are known and expected. For new development, ask business users to help test what that has been done. Involving a wider team (on a volunteer, not a demand, basis) can bring more understanding to timelines and necessity of projects.

Self-Service Impacts with Technology

As we discussed in the chapter on process, with self-service, users expect that a well-defined BA infrastructure with guidelines in place can support their ability to essentially "do it yourself" in terms of analytics, without the help of IT or formal Business Analytics intervention.

Instead of engaging BA and IT teams in the time-consuming tasks of architecting and building analytics, the self-serve model enables the *users* themselves to create and maintain the information they need. In theory, once configured, the self-serve model slides out from beneath the domain of the analytics experts and the IT departments and resides in the domain of the line-of-business and the users, eliminating overhead costs and reporting complexity.

However, self-serve functionality also imposes different requirements on the Business Analytics Program and IT departments that need to be considered to appropriately configure and maintain the source data warehouse, identify the key metrics, and maintain an ever-expanding infrastructure of master and metadata. Moreover, self-serve Business Analytics can place incredible demands on the hardware and software infrastructure if the user community is not well-trained and monitored for appropriate use. Some key shortcomings include:

- Performance bottlenecks as user adoption increases, placing ever-weightier burdens on the hardware infrastructure.
- Uncontrolled growth of custom reports, leading to the fragmentation of information.

- Poorly designed reports that misconstrue information or inaccurately report erroneous information.
- Poorly designed reports that result in poor SQL and impact infrastructure resources.
- Loose governance of the master, dimensional, and metadata that confuses rather than enlightens management or creates compliance issues.
- An influx of uncontrolled, unsanctioned software utilities that can't pass the enterprise standards for security, compliance, and/or maintenance.
- The fragmentation of methods and processes used to support LOB decision making. In addition, multiple users may create different sets of information to answer the same questions.

So, despite the promise of self-serve Business Analytics, all of these caveats *require* the Business Analytics Program and IT to be involved in the creation of the BA infrastructure, the adequate testing and evaluation of the Business Analytics tools, the institution of governance standards and best practices, and the continual monitoring of how the infrastructure is being utilized. A strong governance program will assist in creating success for self-service by supporting the new requirements that are created.

Nonetheless, a self-serve BA infrastructure is clearly a step in maturity that many organizations are mastering: It offers the potential to increase productivity and flatten complexity for users in the technology infrastructure while raising the user adoption levels that denote Business Analytics success. As self-service evolves, the technical teams need to evolve to support it, and it needs to evolve side-by-side with a governance program.

Converging Capabilities and Technology

The majority of our organizations began a maturation process of their Business Analytics journeys in an effort to control costs and maximize efficiencies in the use of Business Analytics. Some began this journey within their individual IT departments. Others became established entities through the direct fiat of management as a separate area within the enterprise.

Regardless of the starting point, all of our Business Analytics Programs have a direct relationship to the IT infrastructure and the technologies that are sustained there. In fact, in IBM's recent survey[5], when asked "What is the key requirement for achieving efficient lifecycle management?" nearly 69 percent of respondents said that line of business, Business Analytics teams, and IT *must* collaborate to achieve success.

This means that the capabilities of Business Analytics must be tied to the convergence requirements of IT to provide adequate capabilities, access, throughput, and support to enable BA users to obtain their required information in a timely and accurate fashion.

---

[5] IBM/Cognos Survey of BICC Sites, 2011.

But this journey of convergence is never complete, and newer technologies offer amazing potential benefits for the organization, refreshing the ecosystems of information while strengthening business management capabilities.

Creating a vibrant, robust technology strategy that includes innovation while protecting investments are key requirements of this collaboration among the Business Analytics team, line-of-business users, and IT. Empowering the user community will remain a measure of achievement. But establishing a realistic balance of support, structure, and cost efficiency will be the ultimate hallmarks of this collaboration's success.

In the next few pages, we look at a case study on how IT and business teams worked together to identify a problem and select technologies to provide the solution, growing their portfolio of analytic offerings to satisfy the business needs. We then review a glossary of technologies available for analytic capabilities and close this chapter with a checklist to consider when working with the "Technology" key to Business Analytics Program Success.

Case Study on Technology: Elie Tahari

From guest author Nihad Aytaman,
Director of Business Applications, Elie Tahari

*International fashion brand manages design-led changes and
five-month production cycles using Business Analytics*

"By using Business Analytics to understand sales patterns, match buying
to sales, increase sell-through, and cut returns, we gain a dramatic return
on investment."

—Nihad Aytaman, Director of Business Applications, Elie Tahari

Elie Tahari Overview

Elie Tahari turned a 1970s startup boutique on Madison Avenue into an international fashion design business, with presence in all upscale department stores and more than 600 boutiques around the world. The firm aims to fuel the global demand for high fashion and quality apparel. But the rapid evolution of the company created numerous challenges to its business objectives.

Elie Tahari needed its full range of designs and sizes available in all of its 35 retail stores. The legacy systems in place did not provide the needed insight into store-specific sales patterns, resulting in stores not being stocked to match their clientele.

Overstocking and retail returns in the fashion industry is a common challenge for apparel manufacturers. Overstocking increases the cost of merchandise through unnecessary shipping and handling. It leads to unsold merchandise and returns to the producer from the retail outlets. These unsold items must then be sold at a lower price to discounting chain stores. The result of this dynamic is a lower profit margin for the company.

"We are 'high fashion,' and designers constantly change and tweak the garments, which means we are always late in production and rushing to get it in store," recalls Nihad Aytaman, Director of Elie Tahari Business Applications. "Due to lack of visibility of x-factory dates tied to customer delivery commitments, we were shipping most of our goods via air freight as opposed to ocean freight. Supplying all these sizes as they ran out became a costly logistics nightmare, and if you consider that air freight is three times more expensive than ocean, it was a very expensive nightmare."

Driving Improvements with Business Analytics Technology

Elie Tahari believed that the key to controlling this overstocking-and-return cycle was to match design production to predictive models of demand. But to create a predictive model, the company needed tighter feedback from its retail stores. This feedback, coupled with historical sales data for each store, could potentially predict customer size and style requirements based on individual store trends.

Unfortunately, the store sales data was slow to arrive at headquarters. The result was that stocks of specific designs and sizes could run out before Elie Tahari knew to send replenishments. And because manufacturing occurred globally, emergency restocking created higher shipping costs as production departments sprinted to meet unpredicted demand.

When the company fully understood how the overstock/availability dynamic was impacting its bottom line, Elie Tahari set specific goals to address the complex problem. These goals were:

- Tune purchasing, manufacturing, inventory, and logistics to match actual sales
- Cut costs through supply chain efficiency, lowering inventory, and reducing returns
- Ensure that every customer has the opportunity to find garments in the chosen design and size at the retail outlet

Aytaman recalls, "The simple solution would have been to over-produce each style and distribute them to every retail outlet. Then the store could always stock every size. But the costs of the excess inventory would kill the business. So we began looking for a way to base inventory levels on what would actually sell."

To achieve these goals, Elie Tahari began to study the problem using Business Analytics tools.

"We built an analytics model that could predict sales volumes on the shop floor and the inventory levels needed to meet those volumes," says Aytaman. "It was based on three years' historic data, current inventory, known production plans, and future orders. The information generated by our predictive model could help us adjust production so that we could have the sizes on hand that the department stores were about to order from us."

Using Technology That Meets the Business and User Needs

The Elie Tahari Business Analytics team then began a step-by-step process to implement the new system. Instead of "boiling the ocean" to deliver an all-encompassing enterprise system, the team worked closely with its business partners to identify what capabilities were needed and to deliver in a series of smaller successes that would continually build momentum while satisfying user needs. They then expanded this across the business with standard technologies and process.

"To solve the challenges of extracting information, starting in 2005 we built a business information warehouse that would act as a single container for our data," Aytaman says. "On top, we deployed a business reporting system that could give us a unified view of operations using Business Intelligence."

Aytaman and a business analyst toured departments asking for "the three to five reports that you can't live without and you want day-in, day-out." For the first department—accounting and finance—it took about six months to create underlying infrastructure, generate the reports, train the users, and prove the system. Once those initial reports were running, the team moved on, and the remainder of the company was moved to the Business Analytics solution within a year. This system covered sales, merchandising, purchasing, production, customer service, accounting, logistics, and company-owned retail stores. Elie Tahari then went live with the Business Intelligence system at the end of 2006 and with its predictive analytics solution in July 2010 to help fulfill the department stores' promise to customers.

"After we deployed Business Analytics, we could correlate shipping with our commitments to customers," reports Aytaman. "This allowed the logistics team to answer the question, 'Do they have time to boat it, or do they have to air it?'"

"With Business Analytics, we have come down to less than 60 percent of shipments by air freight," Aytaman continues. "Because ship freight is more than three times cheaper than air freight, savings amount to millions of dollars annually and have paid for the Business Analytics solution multiple times over within our five years' usage."

Partnership Between Business and IT

"Everybody was using our Business Analytics solutions," says Aytaman, "so we circled back and asked, 'Now that you are using analytics and you have these reports in your possession, what else would you need?' It was like an avalanche! Once people understood what Business Analytics could do for them and what kind of information they could get out of it, they had so many requests, and usage snowballed from there."

Elie Tahari currently has more than 700 reports designed for its 150 users. These users access these reports, on average, around six times a day—a total of 26,000 times a month.

As Nihad Aytaman comments, "We built our data warehouse to be near real-time. Everything that happens within our transactional system flows into the data warehouse within five minutes or less, which explains the very high usage figure. Every time people pull up the same screen, the system provides refreshed data, and so users access these reports throughout the day to look at availability, inventory levels, production levels, and more."

> "We now use Business Analytics Budgeting and Planning to manage the information from store sales to business forecasting, and the sales data is available—automatically—on Monday morning as opposed to Wednesdays. Business Analytics has given us a two-day gain in reacting to the business."
>
> —*Nihad Aytaman*

Aligning Technology to the Business

The use of the Business Analytics tools extends to the individual high-fashion retail stores, helping managers to match their purchasing to sales and thus reducing returns on unsold garments.

Aytaman says, "If you go into a boutique and you look for your size and it's not there, it's very frustrating. After we put Business Analytics in place, one of our regional coordinators said, 'This is a great system,' and I was a little taken aback as users do not usually like new systems. She explained that she was now able to see a discrepancy in the way she was buying for the stores and the way the sizes were selling.

"Business Analytics makes the sales patterns visible, with clear graphical displays. The result was that she adjusted her buying patterns based on what was actually selling," Aytaman continues. "With the right merchandise on the floor, you will sell more. Because you sell more, you diminish returns and reduce reverse logistics costs. Out-of-season merchandise can only be sold to a discount department store, cutting into margins. By using Business Analytics to understand sales patterns—matching buying to sales and increasing sell-through while we cut returned items—we gain a dramatic return on investment."

Technology Best Practices at Elie Tahari

Elie Tahari demonstrated various best practices to accelerate analytics maturity and adoption of the technology in the organization:

- ✓ Technology goals were completely aligned to business outcomes that needed to be achieved. Team members were interviewed and consulted to understand how they would best use the technology and were given the right training and tools to match their needs.
- ✓ Projects were deployed as a series of wins based on value—in terms of business outcomes in consultation with the business partners. This led to very little interference with politics or culture; employees—even down to the store floor—were willing to adopt a new technology because they could quickly understand the value it would provide to them.
- ✓ The central Business Analytics team worked collaboratively in partnership with every area of the business that was involved to ensure the technologies that were implemented were suitable to the user needs and were deployed correctly and in an agile fashion.
- ✓ Acceleration of technology was swift because the capabilities used were matched to the needs of the users and the business outcomes. From a desire to ensure that the Information Management infrastructure was in place to using Business Intelligence and predictive analytics, each technology was valued and adopted.

✓ Technology was thought through—from the analytic capability level to the Information Management level—to ensure a successful deployment that would increase adoption. Confidence in the data and access to the right sources was considered due to the strong partnership between IT and business.

Proven Business Benefits

By adopting a comprehensive Business Analytics Strategy and harnessing both historical and predictive analytics, Elie Tahari has transformed its supply chain, making significant year-on-year savings by aligning manufacturing and logistics more accurately to demand.

Table 7 lists the benefits and impacts of Elie Tahari's new system.

Business area	Benefits	Business impact
Manufacturing and inventory	Enabled successful prediction of sales patterns at different stores 22 weeks into the future to optimize manufacturing and reduced total inventory levels	Expanded program to add two additional retailers
Logistics	Reduced proportion of goods imported by air freight from more than 80 percent to less than 60 percent	Dramatically reduced total inbound freight costs
Packing	Enabled detailed monitoring of efficiencies in the packing department	Improved productivity by 20 percent
Sales	Optimized product mix at each store and accelerated response to changing fashion trends	10 percent of total sales growth is estimated to result from analytics

Table 7: Results Achieved with Elie Tahari's Business Analytics System

The technology solution was mapped directly to the users' needs and embraced by the organization because it made their jobs easier and improved the performance of the company's employees and retail representatives. The IT team sought feedback from the users in an effort to improve the technology solution, and the close partnership between the various teams resulted in success.

Practical Tips: Selecting Technologies for Your Business Analytics Needs

In the preceding chapter, we discussed business analytics technologies and considerations when deploying analytics. Let's review these technologies and offer a glossary around each of them that many of us have considered in a portfolio of standards.

As a simple overview of the technologies involved, Figure 28 shows the broad categories of solutions. Each of these categories contains a number of different technologies that serve different purposes.

Business Intelligence	Performance Management	Predictive Analytics	Risk Analytics
Information Management and Governance			
Information Integration	Data Management	Data Warehouse	Data Quality
Deployment Options			
Enterprise Software | Virtualization | Optimized Business Systems | Cloud			

Figure 28: Categories of Technology Solutions

Business Analytics

Business Intelligence: Business Intelligence capabilities typically include reporting, dashboards, scorecards, and analysis. They may also involve real-time, what-if scenario analysis and statistical analysis. These tools allow historical, current and future views of information and can turn data into insight that will aid in decision making. Business Intelligence tools are relatively easy to use and are helpful for wide user adoption to assist in users' decision-making ability, whether it is creating new reports and analysis or receiving at-a-glance views of dashboards or scorecards.

Performance Management: Performance Management solutions typically consist of planning, forecasting, analysis, profitability modeling, financial close management, performance reporting, scorecarding, and enterprise disclosure management. These solutions can help drive profitable growth and address regulation and risk. They help identify performance gaps, track performance against corporate objectives, and let users assess alternatives while replacing rigid budgets with continuous planning and forecasting.

Predictive Analytics: Predictive analytics enables users to predict what will happen next in order to make better decisions for future outcomes. With predictive analytics, you can perform advanced analytics, data mining, text mining, social media analytics, and statistical analysis, including regression analysis, cluster analysis, correlation analysis, data collection, online survey research, data modeling, and predictive modeling.

Risk Analytics: Risk analytics supports risk analysis and insight and helps achieve compliance with regulations such as Dodd-Frank, Basel II/III, Solvency II, and more. It can help to reduce credit losses, manage operational risk, and more.

Information Management and Governance

Information Management and Governance capabilities allow organizations to gain confidence in their data. There are a variety of tools in this category, such as information integration capabilities that let users connect, understand, cleanse, transform, deliver, or replicate data. These solutions provide the ability to deliver authoritative, consistent, timely, and complete information and govern its quality throughout its lifecycle. There are also Master Data Management solutions that enable organizations to centrally and physically manage and maintain master data for multiple domains. Data Management and Data Warehousing solutions include storage, administration, design, and development. They are also the category of platforms or appliances that deliver access to structured and unstructured information or may combine storage, processing, and database.

Deployment Options

Deployment options are the various types of deployment methodologies that are used to suit different needs. These can include enterprise software, virtualization, workload-optimized systems, and cloud solutions.

While this list may not be completely comprehensive of all solutions on the market today, it provides an overview of the main categories of solutions that should be considered as part of the Business Analytics Program that will help you achieve success with a large number of users and reach higher levels of analytic maturity. Evaluation of new innovations should occur regularly throughout the program journey to continually introduce analytic inventions that will achieve better business outcomes that are right for your organization.

Technology Checklist

In the Technology chapter, we discussed a number of considerations for your Business Analytics Program to deploy technology in a way that can help create efficiencies while maintaining agility and introducing innovation. Use this checklist to see which areas might be useful to integrate and manage over time in your organization:

- ✓ Have you assessed how your stakeholders need to use technology to turn information into insights that can better inform decision making?
- ✓ Have you considered a Line-of-Business Domain model within the Center of Excellence that can assist with technology selection?
- ✓ Do your solutions let your users view information in the various time horizons needed (past, present, future)?
- ✓ Have you considered a set of standards for the various technology capabilities required?
- ✓ Have you been architecting your solution with user adoption and growth in mind?
- ✓ Are you tightly connected with the Information Management team to ensure confidence in information?
- ✓ Have you considered the variety of deployment options to select what best fits your organization today and in the future?
- ✓ How are you proactively evaluating and introducing new innovations into your analytic capability standards?
- ✓ Are you architecting your solution to promote self-service?
- ✓ Are you considering future performance and scalability as well as administration as your solution matures and grows adoption?

Conclusion

In this book, we have identified, sometimes through trial and error, the 5 Keys that we believe are critical to Business Analytics Program success. However, for those who are just starting on their Business Analytics journey, it must be realized that these keys are often improved during the analytics journey and it is through small wins over time that your program will grow. However, by considering these 5 Keys—or elements—early in your journey, you can rapidly accelerate the success of the program in your organization.

While the elements are not necessarily put in place in the order described in this book, they are all interconnected and often hard to separate. Without a strategy, it is difficult to instill the vision and create the roadmap for analytic success. The strategy will determine the value outcomes that need to be monitored and measured over time to continually prove value. The proof of value will allow the organizational support to grow and gain user adoption and an analytic culture that will help the program move forward. To achieve this progress, processes that create efficiencies and maintain agility must be put in place, and it all needs to be underpinned with the right technology solutions that will help to achieve better decision making that will produce the desired outcomes of the organization.

Over time, different areas of the business may fall into different levels of maturity as each area onboards into the program. This is to be expected. When looking at an organization, if you view the different departments as an example (or it might be domain or business areas), you can see that each department should be looking at whether they are able to gain visibility into information across all time horizons (present, past, future) as necessary (Figure 29).

Figure 29: Departmental View of Information

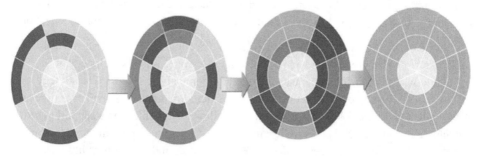

Figure 30: Departmental Maturation over Time

Figure 30 shows how a maturation might occur over time as the roadmap is created in the strategy to improve analytics in each area. In the last stage depicted, the outcome achieves the Master maturity level defined by the AQ Maturity Model.

As the Business Analytics Program matures over time, each department may go through its own maturity levels. As they deliver value on the analytics that are produced, each will grow and strive for the next outcome. The maturity level of each of the 5 Keys can be mapped against the model shown in Figure 31 for each area to determine where improvements need to be made and what steps the Business Analytics Program can take to help the teams improve in their own areas.

At the heart of it are the people involved—and the Analytics Center of Excellence that supports the program and drives the culture. The Center of Excellence can be the team that drives change—and manages this change to achieve engagement, buy-in, and change. This cannot be done without team engagement but most important is executive involvement. Executive involvement may naturally occur with a top analytic executive—perhaps a Chief Analytics Officer—something we are seeing as an emerging executive role in the industry. The Chief Analytics Officer can create and execute on the strategy, create business value, organize people, and introduce the processes and technologies necessary to achieve the goals of the organization.

However, it is not a project—it is a *program*. It is not a destination—it is a *journey*. As user adoption grows, needs change, technology innovation continues, and the organization will continue to improve and test the boundaries over time. Change needs to be continually managed and introduced, and the program will need continual improvement.

The insights in this book have been derived from the combined experiences of 10 organizations that are on the analytic journey. While we may be in higher levels of maturity today, we still continue to advance on the journey and have a robust program in place

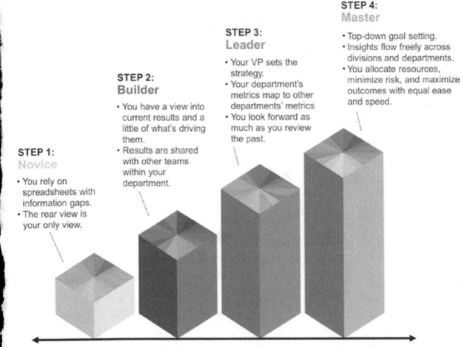

Figure 31: The Analytics Quotient Maturity Model

to support it. It took many years to develop a program, and that program will continue to change and grow over time.

By sharing the 5 Keys to Business Analytics Program Success, we hope that organizations in the industry will learn and implement some best practices that will help them accelerate success in their own analytics journey. We will all look forward to the technology evolution with a strong program foundation that allows us to be ready to continually achieve excellence in the future.